VOCAL SOLO

VOLUME 2

Re

MW00896830

Kids' Musical Theatre Collection

Kids' Musical Theatre Collection

To access audio visit:
www.halleonard.com/mylibrary

Enter Code
2524-8295-5071-1849

ISBN 978-1-4234-8332-8

7777 W. BLUEMOUND RD. P.O. BOX 13819 MILWAUKEE, WI 53213

HAL LEONARD HAS MANY BOOKS OF SOLOS FOR CHILDREN

TABLE OF CONTENTS

The price of this publication includes access to companion recorded accompaniments online, for download or streaming, using the unique code found on the title page. Visit **www.halleonard.com/mylibrary** and enter the access code.

BABY MINE

from Walt Disney's *Dumbo*

Words by Ned Washington
Music by Frank Churchill

C/E Dm7 C G9sus C G/B Am Am/G
mine. Lit - tle one when you
F6 Fm6 Fm6/G G7 C G/B Am Am/G
play don't you mind what they
F6 Fm6 Fm6/G G7 F F/E Dm7 Dm7/C
say. Let those eyes spar - kle and
F6 Fdim C/E Dm7 C E7
shine, nev - er a tear, ba - by of mine.

Somewhat faster
Am
Bm7
E7sus
E7
If they knew sweet lit - tle you,
Am
Bm7
E7sus
E7
they'd end up lov - ing you too.
Am
Am/C
Em
Em/G
Am
Am/G
All those same peo - ple who scold you, what they'd
F♯m7♭5
B7
Em
B/D♯
Dm7
G7
C
G/B
give just for the right to hold you. From your

Am Am/G F6 Fm6 Fm6/G G7 C G/B
head to your toes, you're not
Am Am/G F6 Fm6 Fm6/G G7 F F/E
much, good-ness knows, but you're
Dm7 F6 Fdim G7♭9 C
so pre-cious to me, cute as can be, ba-by of mine.
F6 C F6 C

BE KIND TO YOUR PARENTS

from *Fanny*

Words and Music by
Harold Rome

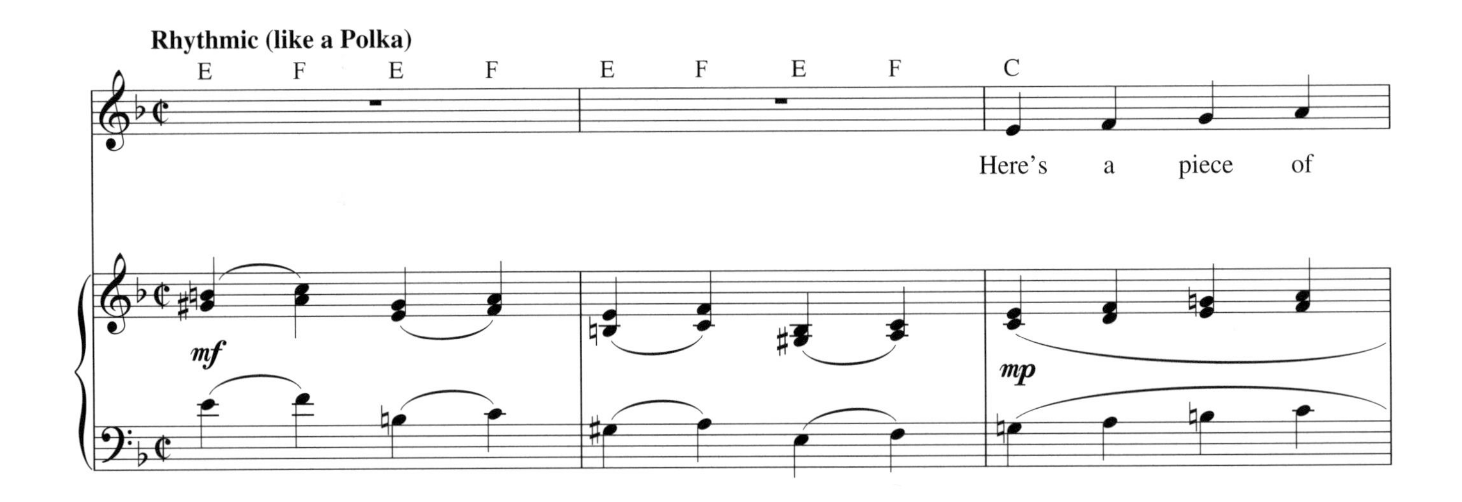

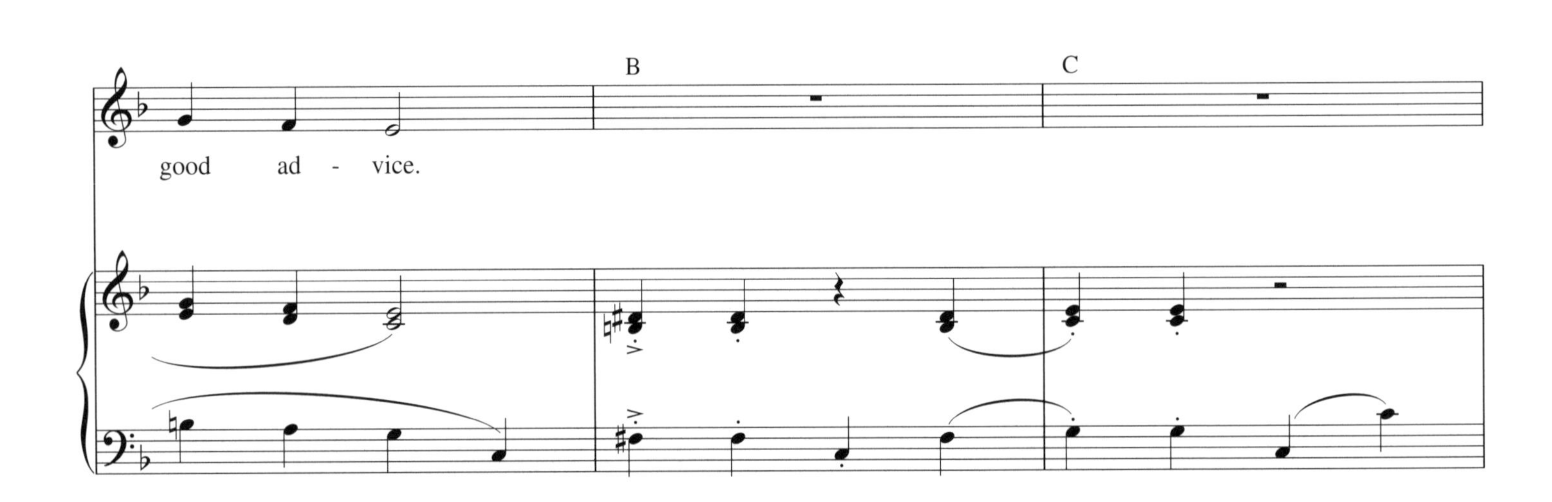

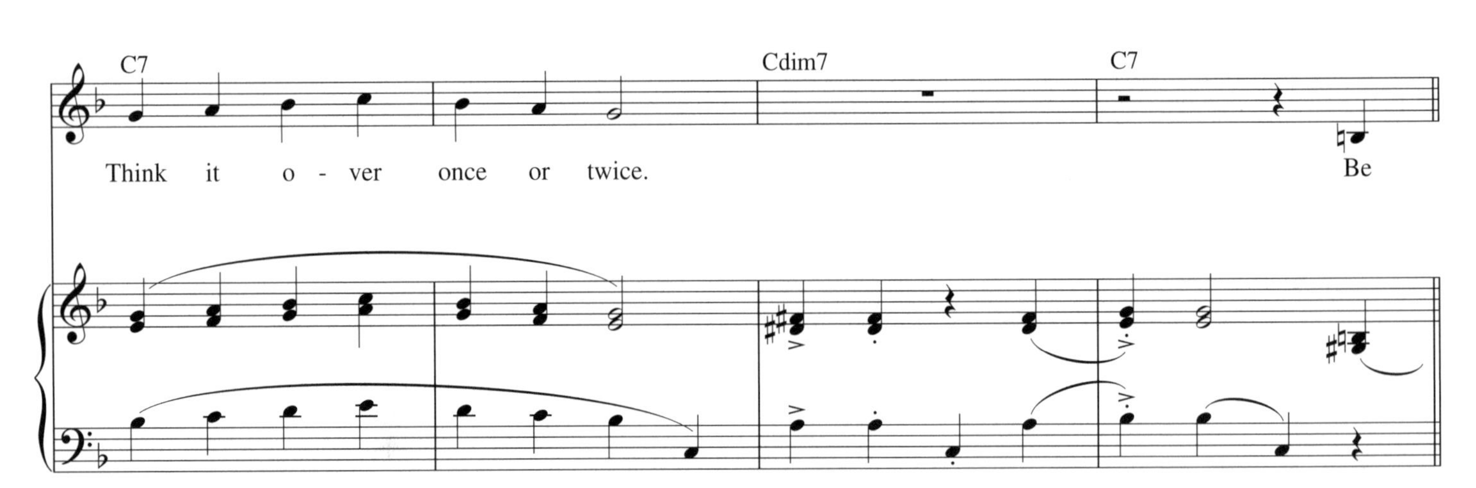

This song is performed by Fanny and Cesario in the show, adapted here as a solo.

F
C7
kind to your par - ents, though they don't de -
mf
serve it. Re - mem - ber they're grown - ups, a
B♭
C7
F
E
F
dif - fi - cult stage of life. They're apt to be
C7
ner - vous, and o - ver - ex - cit - ed, con -

F6 C7 F F7
fused from their dai - ly storm and strife. Just keep in
B♭ F Fdim7 F
mind, though it sounds odd, I know,
mf
B C F♯9 G9
most par - ents once were chil - dren long a -
C Gm C7 E F
go. In - cred - i - ble! So treat them with pa - tience and

C7
sweet un - der - stand - ing, in spite of the
B♭ C7 Fmaj7 F7
fool - ish things they do! Some -
B♭ B♭m C7
day you may wake up and find you're a par - ent,
1 F E F Cdim7 C7
too. Be
2 F E F
too.

BEIN' GREEN

from *Sesame Street*

Words and Music by
Joe Raposo

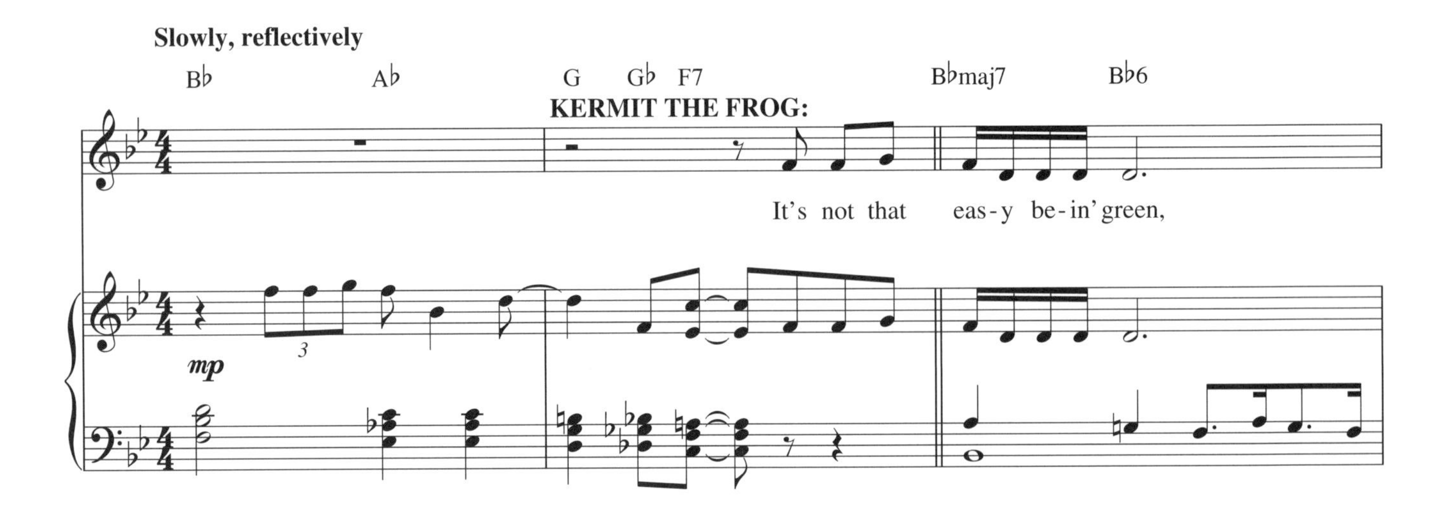

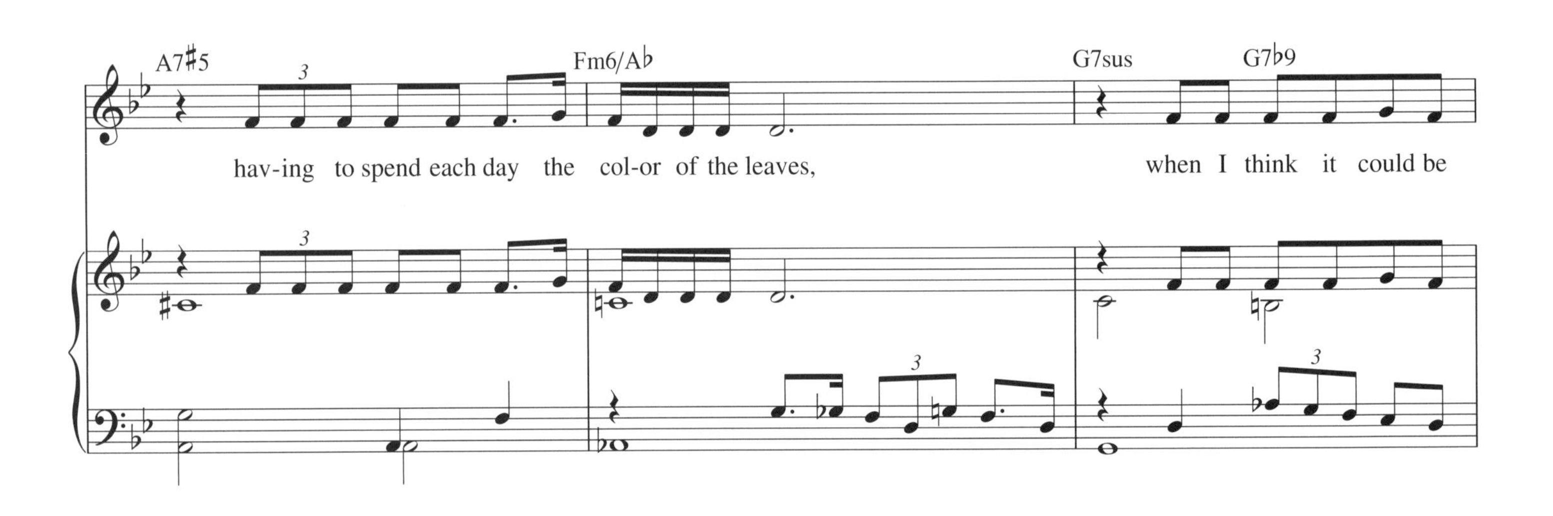

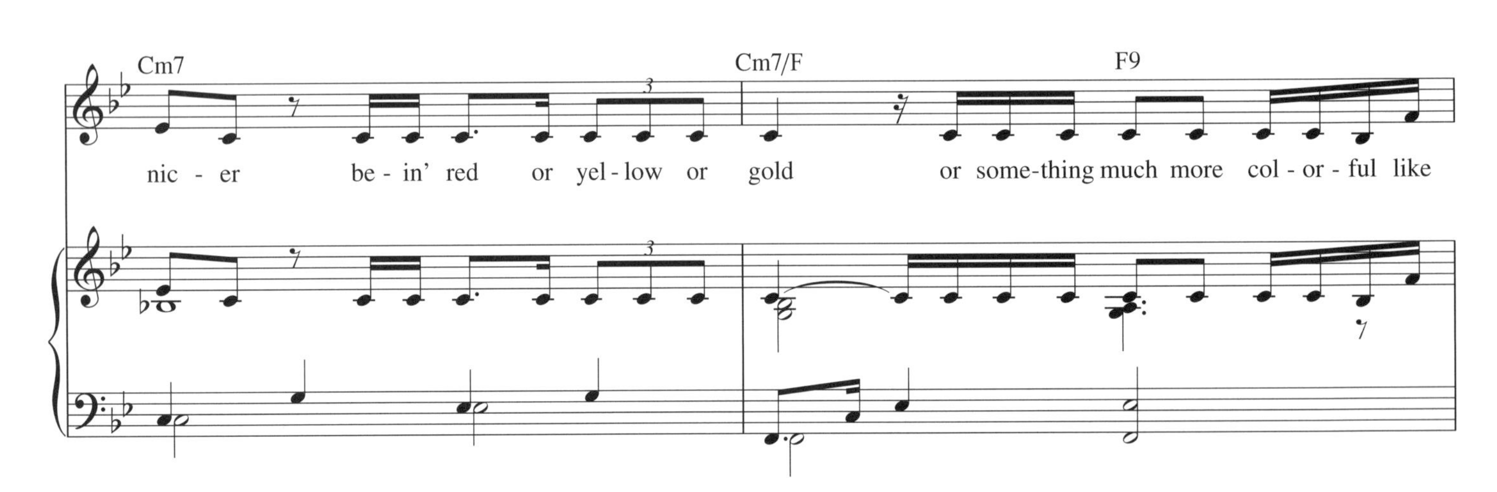

B♭
A♭
G♭
F7
B♭maj7
B♭6
that.
It's not eas-y be-in' green.
A7♯5
Fm6/A♭
It seems you blend in with so man-y oth-er or-di-nar-y things,
G7sus
G7♭9
Cm7
and peo-ple tend to pass you o-ver 'cause you're not stand-ing out like flash-y
Cm7/F
F9
B♭
spar-kles on the wa-ter or stars in the sky.

Dm/A
A♭maj7
But green is the col - or of spring,
cresc.
mf
D♭maj7
B♭
Dm/A
and green can be cool and friend-ly - like,
and green can be
Gm7
Gm(maj7)
Gm7/C
C9
big like an o - cean or im - por - tant like a moun - tain or
cresc.
f
Cm7
Cm7/F
F7
tall like a tree.
When green is
decresc.
mp

B♭maj9
B♭6/9
A7♯5
all there is to be,
it could make you
3
Fm6/A♭
Dm7/G
G7
wonder why, but why wonder, why wonder? I am
3
Cm7
Cm7/F
F9
green, and it'll do fine. It's beautiful, and I think it's
3
B♭
B♭(add2)
what I want to be.
decresc.
pp

DREAM FOR YOUR INSPIRATION

from *The Muppets Take Manhattan*

Words and Music by
Scott Brownlee

G
G/B
C
I used to get to feel - ing so down heart - ed,
I used to think that I was noth - ing spe - cial,
So if you think that you are me - di - o - cre,
I used to e - ven hate the
that I was just an - oth - er
and ev - 'ry - thing you do is
D
col - or green.
pret - ty face.
just so - so,
But ev - 'ry time I think I can't get start - ed, I
But now I know that I will be suc - cess - ful
And if you're wish - in' you could start all o - ver,
To Coda
think of all my dreams and then I'm right back on the beam. You've got to
if I al - ways do just what I real - ly want to do. You've got to
stop and re - al - ize you've got your dreams and you'll be fine. You've got to
dream for your
dream of your
in - spir - a - tion.
se - cret wish - es.
Dream of what you can do, 'cause with your
Dream of your high - est hopes, 'cause if you

G G/B
1
C
D
dreams and some per - spir - a - tion, an - y-thing with-in your dream-ing is with-in your reach.
dream, you can
2
C
D7
B7
make your dreams come true. When you've
Em
B7
Em
fin - 'lly de - cid - ed things aren't as bad as they seem,
A
D
A
A7
D
3
You just can't de - ny it, where there's a will there's a dream. Yeah! You've got to

G G/B C G G/B D
dream for your in - spir - a - tion. Dream of what you can do, 'cause if you
G G/B C D7
dream, you can make your dreams come true. You've got to
G D7 G D7 G D.S. al Coda
dream, dream.
CODA
G G/B
dream for your
C G G/B D
in - spir - a - tion. Dream of what you can do, 'cause with your

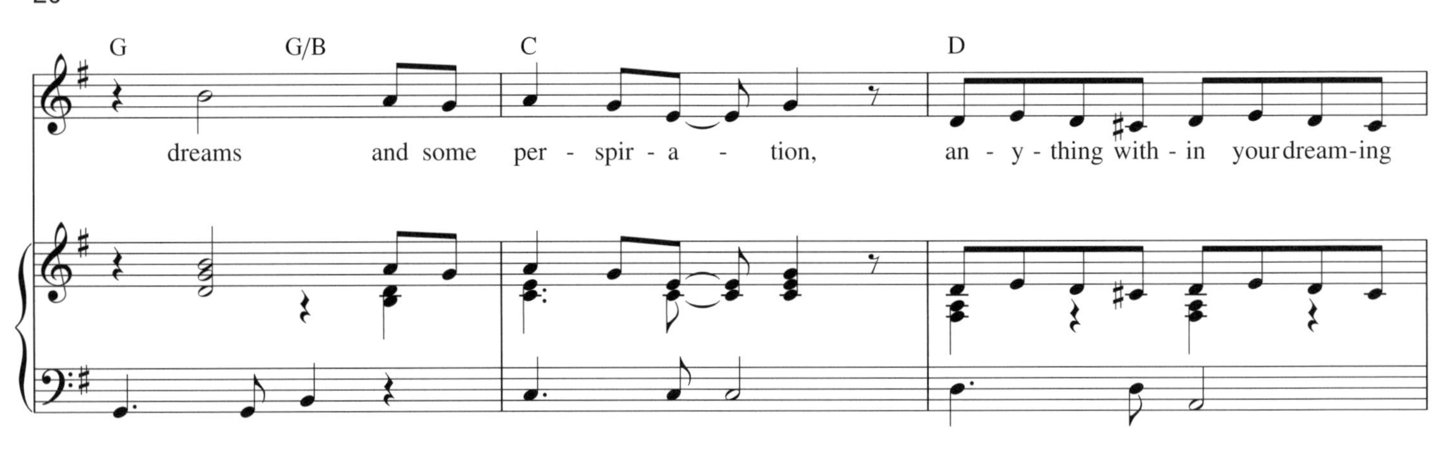
G G/B C D
dreams and some per - spir - a - tion, an - y - thing with - in your dream-ing

G G/B C
is with - in your reach. You've got to dream of your se - cret wish - es.

G G/B D G G/B C
Dream of your high-est hopes, _'cause if you dream, you can make your dreams come

D7 G
true. You've got to dream.

FRIEND

from *Snoopy!!!*

Words by Hal Clayton Hackady
Music by Larry Grossman

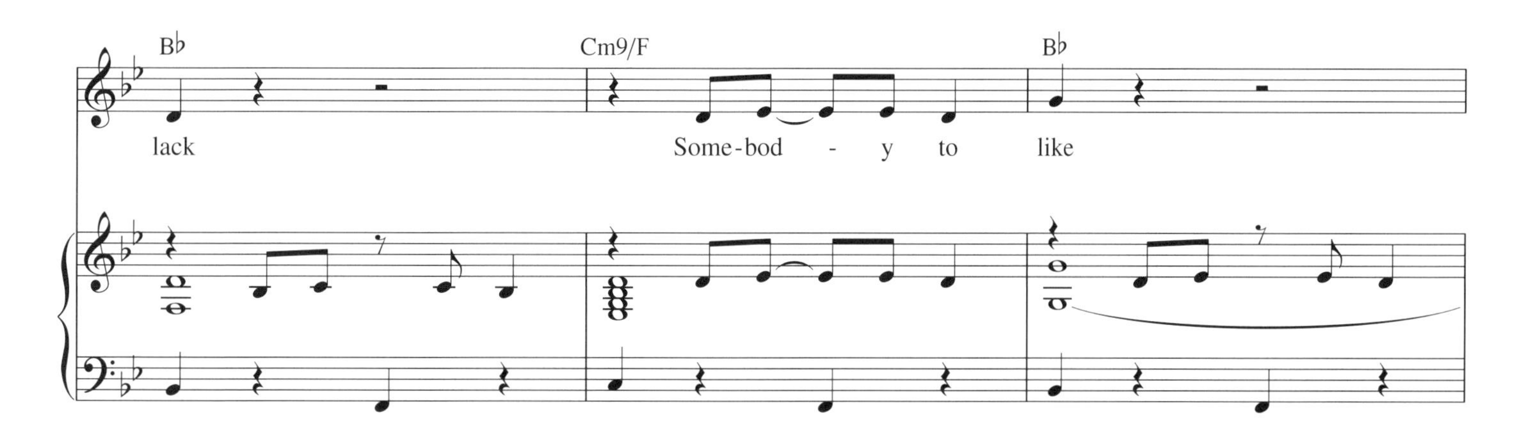

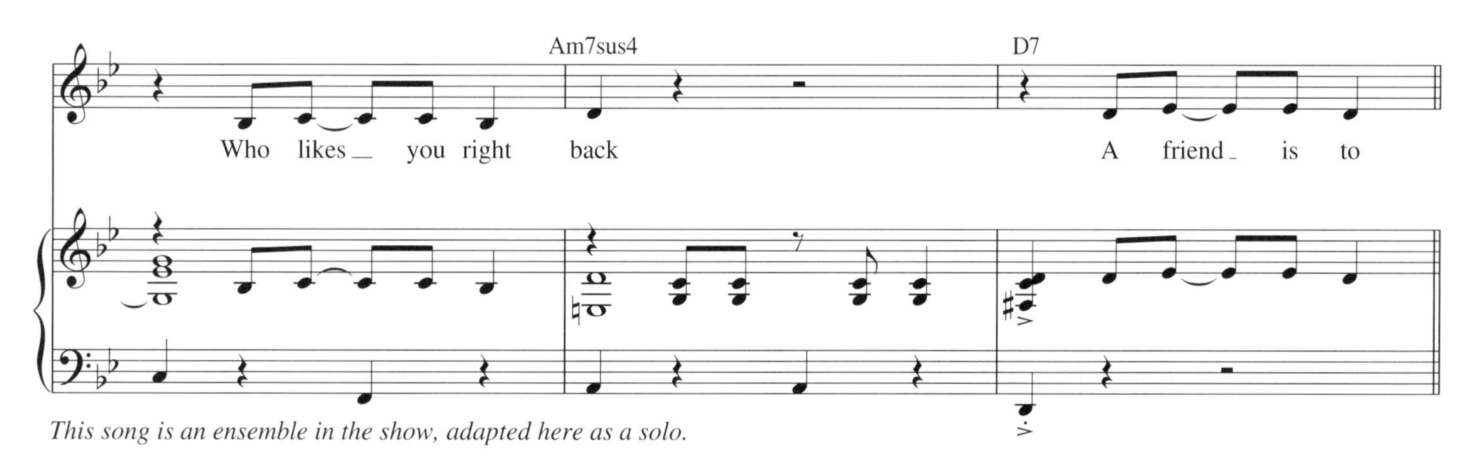

This song is an ensemble in the show, adapted here as a solo.

Gm
C13
please
A friend is to cheer
Cm7/F
F13
F7♯9♭6
To help through the night, A friend is to write: "I wish you were
Dm7sus
C♯dim
Cm9/F
B♭
Cm7/F
here!" A friend is to trust and fight to de-
B♭
Cm9/F
B♭
F13
fend. A friend is a must When you need a

B♭13
B♭(♭13)
E♭maj7/G
E♭m/G♭
friend
You on - ly need one
And friend _ when you
B♭/F
C9
Cm7
Cm7/F
do
Your ver - y best friend, your friend _ to the end had bet - ter be
1
B♭
Cm7/F
B♭
Cm7/F
you.
Had bet - ter be you.
A friend is to
mp
2
B♭
Cm7/F
B♭
you!
ff

GARY, INDIANA

from Meredith Willson's *The Music Man*

By Meredith Willson

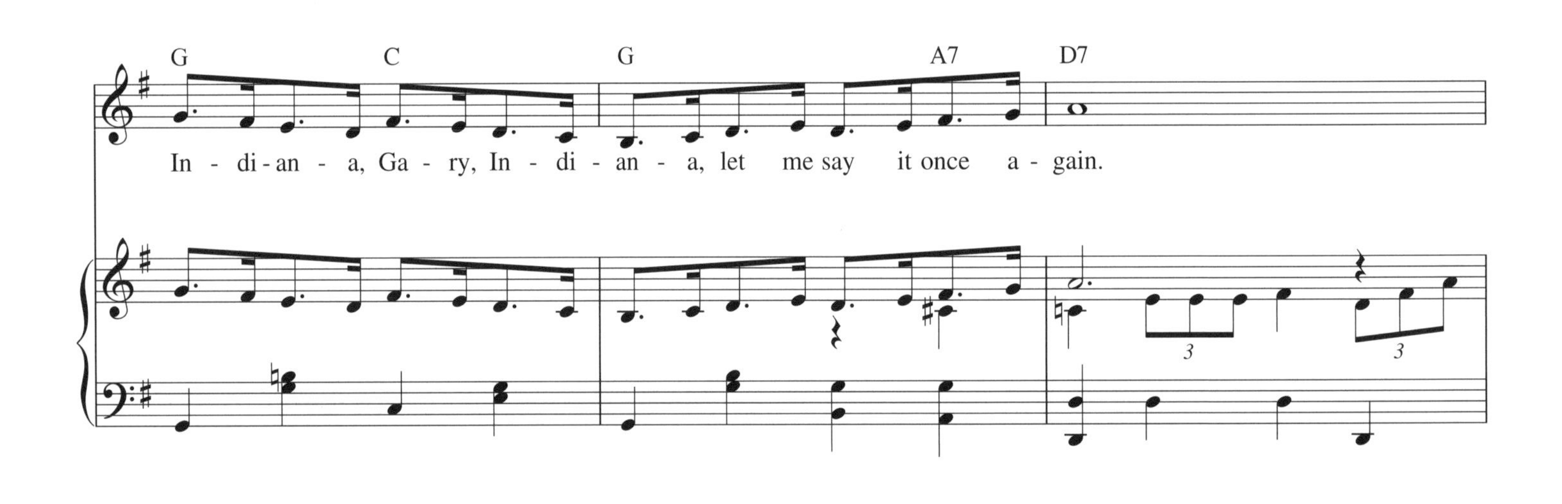

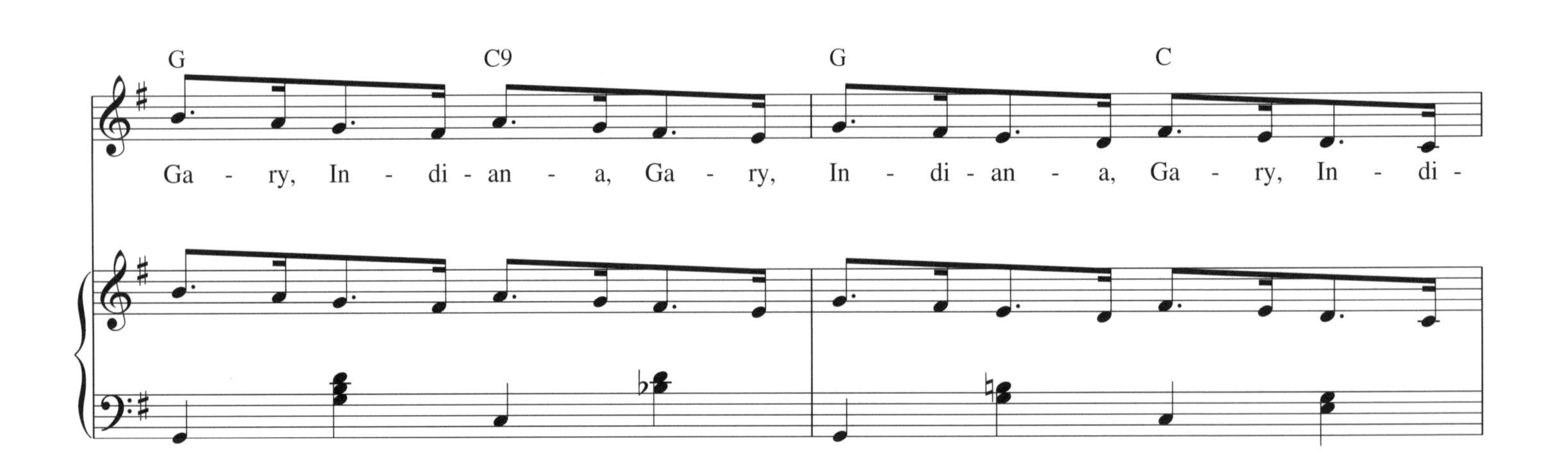

G
D7
G
an - a, that's the town that knew me when.
If you'd
C
G
like to have a log - i - cal ex - pla - na - tion
how I
C
G
hap - pened on this el - e - gant syn - co - pa - tion,
I will
C
G
say with - out a mo - ment of hes - i - ta - tion,
there is

Bm Dm6 E7♯5 A Cm6 D7♯5 G C9
just one place that can light my face. Ga - ry, In - di - an - a, Ga - ry,
G C G D Bm7 Dm6 E7
In - di - an - a, not Lou - i - si - an - a, Par - is, France, New York or Rome, but
A9 D7
Ga - ry, In - di - an - a, Ga - ry, In - di - an - a, Ga - ry, In - di - an - a, my home sweet
1 G G7 2 G E♭7 G D7 G
home. If you'd home.

GETTING TO KNOW YOU

from *The King and I*

Lyrics by Oscar Hammerstein II
Music by Richard Rodgers

This song is an ensemble number in the show, adapted here as a solo.

Edim7 B♭/F G7 Gm7/C Gm7
learn - ing (You'll for - give me if I boast.) And I've now be - come an
C9 Cm7/F F7
(Spoken)
ex - pert On the sub - ject I like most, Get-ting to know you.
Refrain (gracefully and not fast)
B♭ Cm7 F7
Get-ting to know you, get-ting to know all a - bout you
mp
tranquillo
Cm7 F7 Cm7 F7 Cm7 F7 B♭
Get-ting to like you, get-ting to hope you like me

E♭maj7 E♭6
Get-ting to know you, Put-ting it my way, but nice - ly
E♭+ E♭ Gm7 C7 Cm7/F
You are pre-cise - ly My cup of tea!
cresc.
mf
F7 B♭ Cm7 F7
Get-ting to know you, get-ting to feel free and eas - y
f
p
Cm7 F7 Cm7 F7 Cm7 F7 B♭7
When I am with you, get-ting to know what to say.

E♭maj7 E♭6 Cm7 F7
Have-n't you no - ticed? Sud-den-ly I'm bright and
B♭maj7 B♭7 E♭maj7 B♭
breez - y Be - cause of all the
Cm7 F7sus F7 B♭(add9) Gm7 C7 Gm7 C7
beau-ti-ful and new things I'm learn-ing a-bout you
poco a poco cresc.
Cm7 F7 B♭ E♭ B♭
day by day.
mf

GOD HELP THE OUTCASTS

from Walt Disney's *The Hunchback of Notre Dame*

Music by Alan Menken
Lyrics by Stephen Schwartz

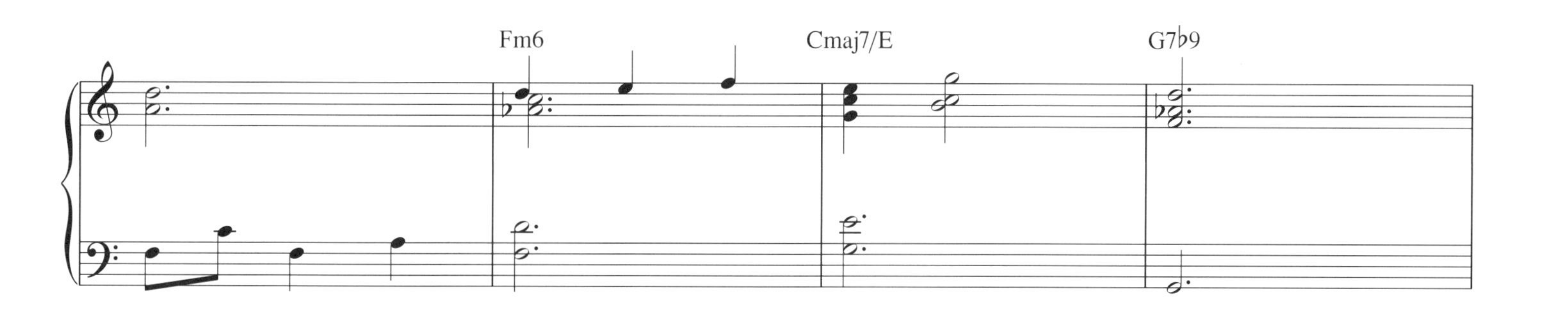

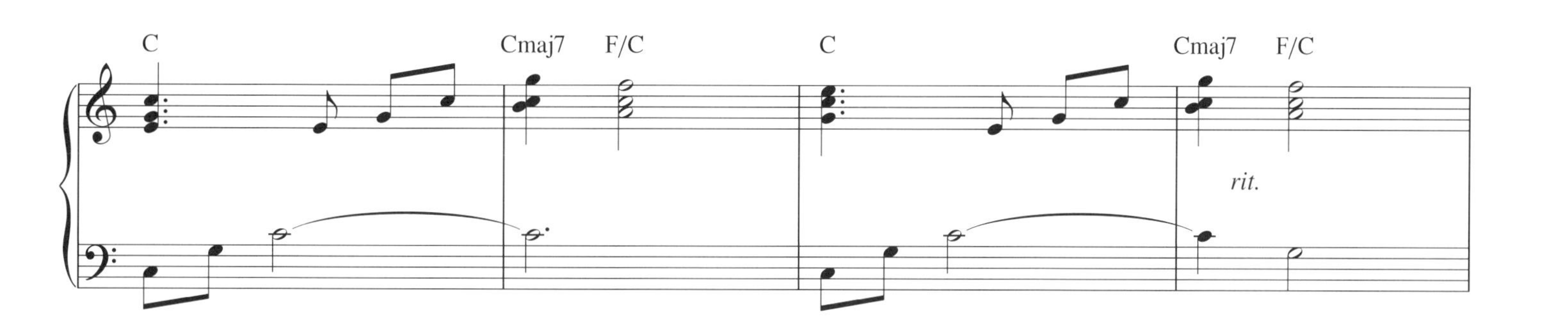

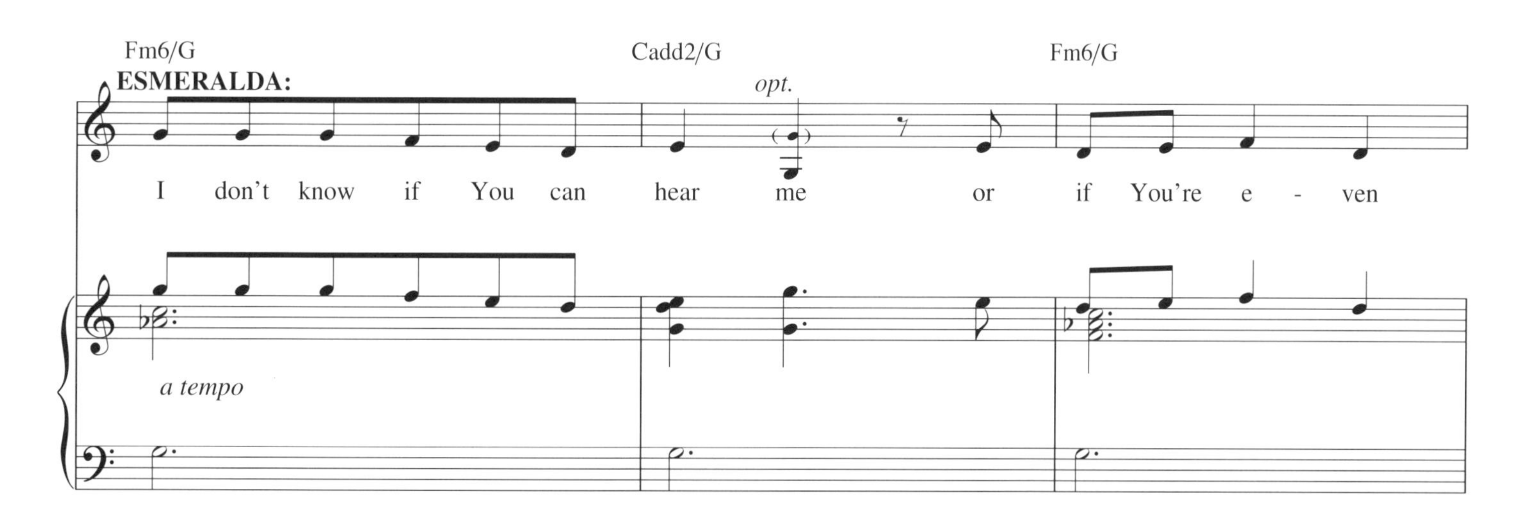

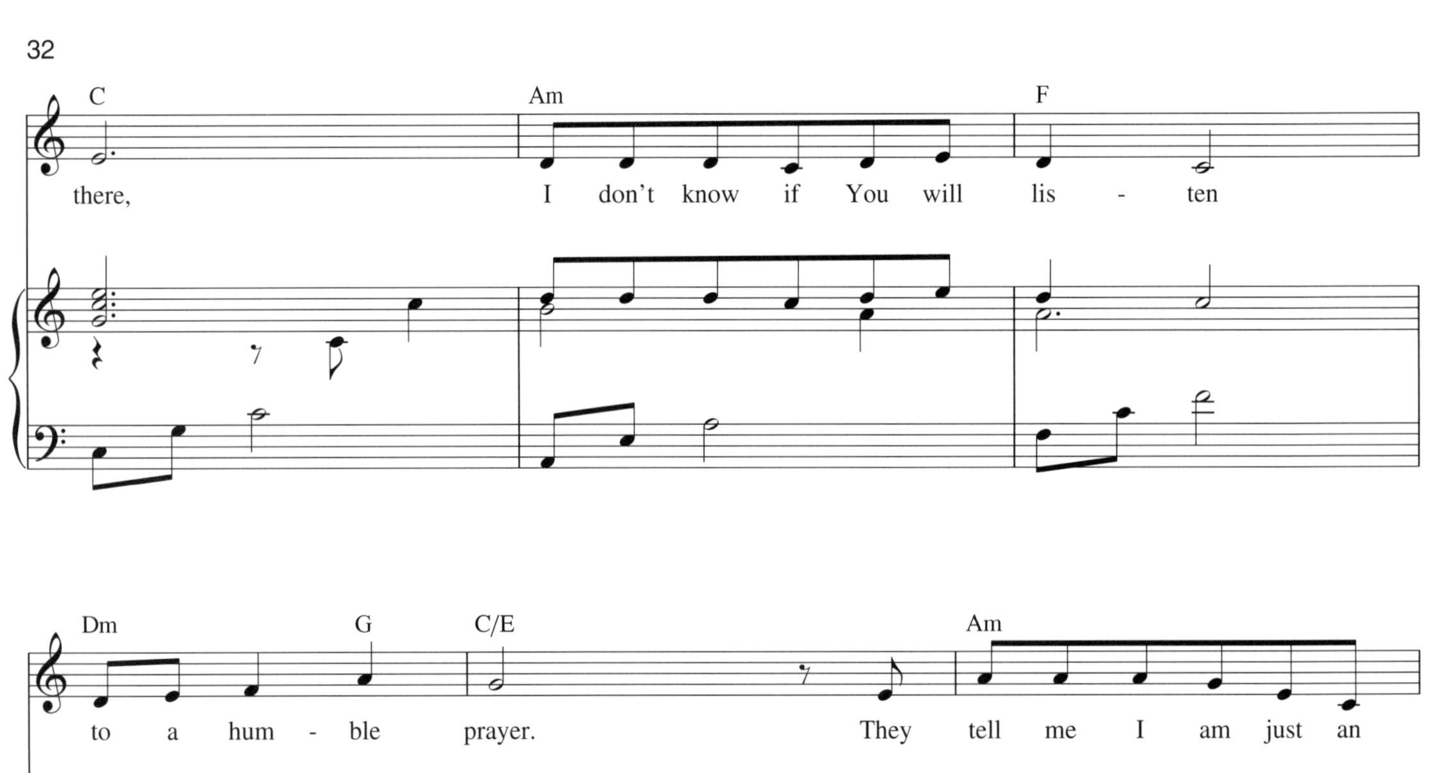
C
Am
F
there,
I don't know if You will lis - ten

Dm
G
C/E
Am
to a hum - ble prayer.
They tell me I am just an

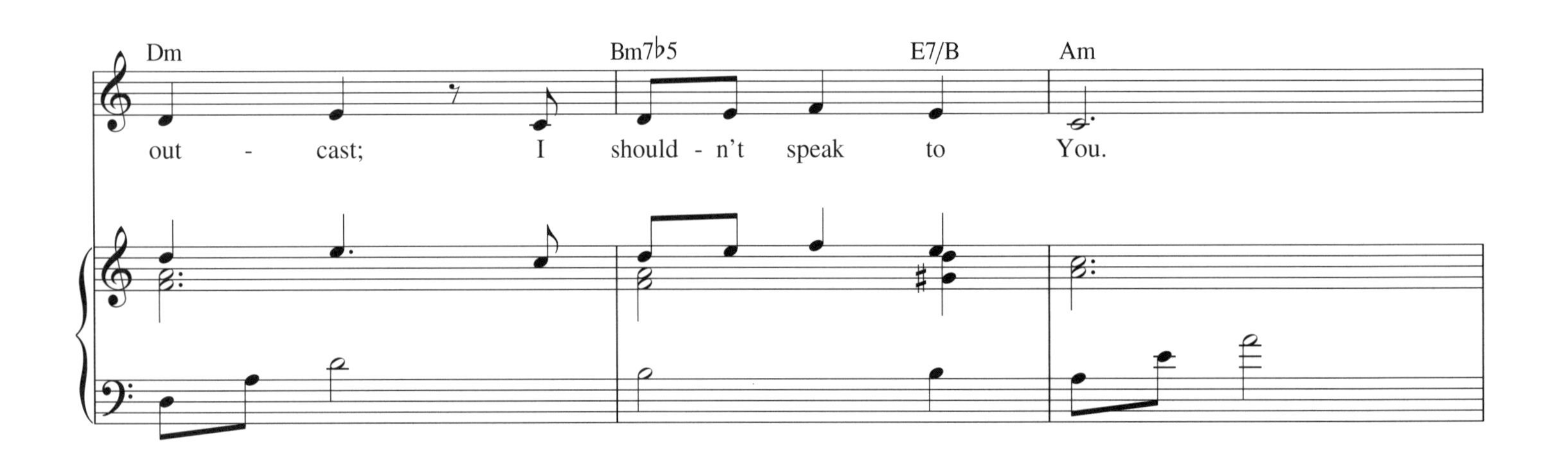
Dm
Bm7♭5
E7/B
Am
out - cast; I should - n't speak to You.

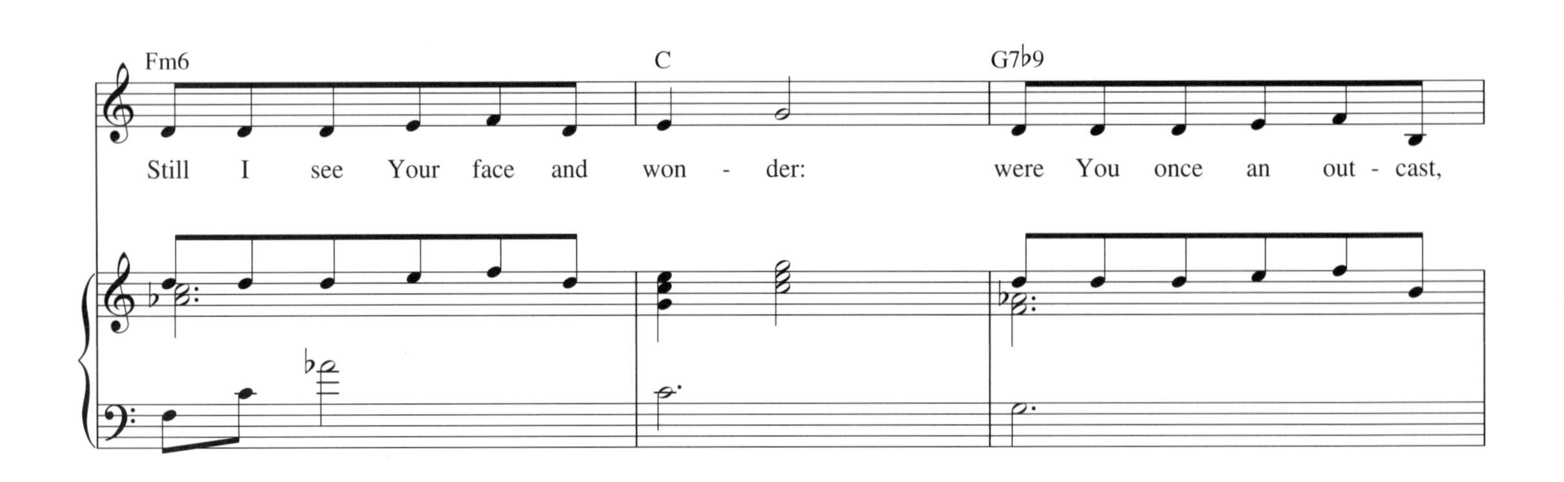
Fm6
C
G7♭9
Still I see Your face and won - der: were You once an out - cast,

C
Cmaj7
F/C
C
Cmaj7
F/C
too?
C
Cmaj7/E
Fadd9
God help the out - casts, hun - gry from
I ask for noth - ing, I can get
mf
Dm7
C/G
G
opt.
birth. Show them the mer - cy they
by. But I know so man - y less
Csus
C
opt.
G/B
Am
don't find on earth. The lost and for -
luck - y than I. God help the

G/A
Dm7
got - ten, they look to You still.
out - casts, the poor and down - trod.
Fm6
C/G
opt.
G7♭9
God help the out - casts or no - bod - y
I thought we all were the chil - dren of
1
C
Cmaj7
F/C
C
G/C
F/C
will.
2
C
G/B
F/A
C/G
opt.
God.
I don't know if there's a rea - son why
mp

Dm/G
C
Em/B
Am
some are blessed, some not.
Why the few You seem to
Fadd9
Dm7
C/E
fa - vor,
they fear us,
flee us
Em
Asus
A
try not to see us.
D
D/F♯
G
God help the out - casts, the tat - tered, the
f

Em
Asus
A
Dsus
D
torn, seek - ing an an - swer to why they were
opt.
A/D
Bm
Em
born. Winds of mis - for - tune have blown them a -
Gm6
D/A
Dmaj7/A
A7♭9
bout. You made the out - casts; don't cast them
decresc.
Bm
Dmaj7/A
Gm6
D/F♯
out. The poor and un - luck - y, the
mp

Gm6
D/F♯
Gm6
D/F♯
Em
weak and the odd;
I thought we
poco rit.
D/F♯
opt.
A7♭9
D
all were the chil - dren of God.
a tempo
Dmaj7
G/D
D
Dmaj7
G/D
Bm
F♯m/A
G6
A
D
rit.

I ALWAYS KNEW

from *Annie Warbucks*

Lyric by Martin Charnin
Music by Charles Strouse
Arranged by Michael Dansicker

16
Dsus4
C/D
D
Gm
Cm7(sus4)
I said my prayers and I would go to sleep be -
mp
19
F7
B♭
E♭
liev - ing I guess the trick is that you
22
Cm7(sus4)
C6/D
C/D
got - ta keep be - liev - ing!
3
26
D7
G
D7sus4
G(add9)
'Cause when you do, there go your tears, there goes_ your dark -
mf

C(add9)
Eb6(add9)
A7b5/Eb
G/D
-est night, and the light breaks through I al-ways hoped, I al-ways
G+/D
C
Cm/Eb
G/D
dreamed, boy, how I hoped, boy how I dreamed, no that ain't true.
GMaj7 G6
Cm6/D
I always knew I al-ways
f
Stringendo
G/B
Eb/Bb
C/A
C/D
Cm/D
G(add9)
knew!
poco rit.
fff

LITTLE PEOPLE

from *Les Misérables*

Music by Claude-Michel Schönberg
Lyrics by Alain Boublil, Jean-Marc Natel
and Herbert Kretzmer

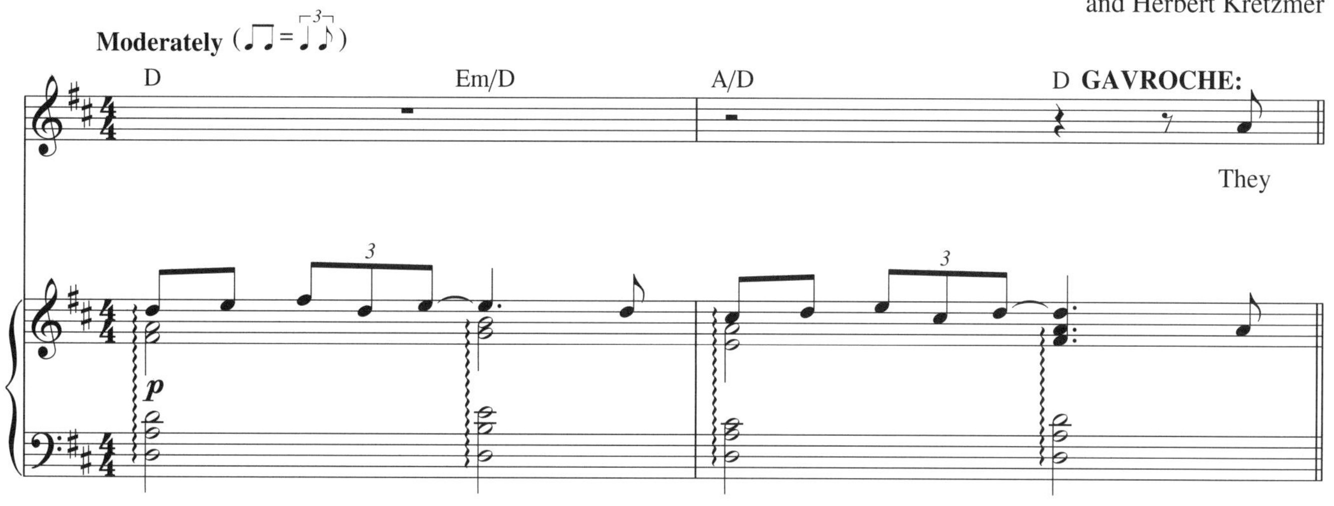

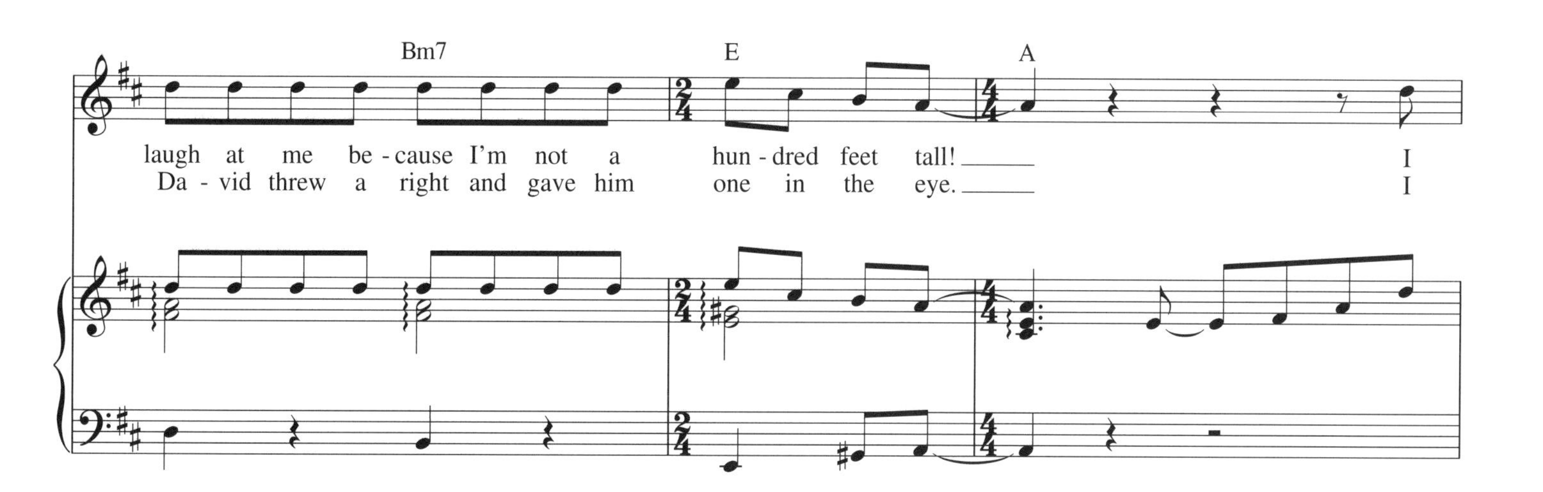

G
Em7
A
D
tell 'em there's a lot to learn down here on the ground.
nev - er read the Bi - ble but I know that it's true.
The
It
D/F♯
A
D
world is big but lit - tle peo - ple turn it a - round.
on - ly goes to show what lit - tle peo - ple can do!
A
Em7
A7
D
worm can roll a stone, a bee can sting a bear, a
Em7
A7
D
fly can fly a - round Ver - sailles 'cos flies don't care!
A

To Coda
D7 G F♯ Bm G Em7
spar-row in a hat can make a hap-py home, a flea can bite the bot-tom of the
1 D/A A7 D
Pope in Rome! Go-
2 D/A A7 B♭
Pope in Rome!
F
So lis-ten here, Pro-fes-sor, with your head in the cloud,
B♭ C
it's of-ten kind of use-ful to get lost in a crowd.

F
Eb
F
So keep your u - ni - ver - si - ties, I don't give a damn;
Bb
F
Bb
for bet - ter or for worse it is the way that I am!
Be
Cm
F
D
care - ful as you go 'cos lit - tle peo - ple grow...
And
Em7
A7
D
lit - tle peo - ple know when lit - tle peo - ple fight we

Em7
A7
D
G
may look eas - y pick-ings but we got some bite! So nev - er kick a dog be -
F♯
Bm
G
Em7
cause it's just a pup. You bet - ter run for cov - er when the
D/A
A/G
D/F♯
3
G
Em7
D/A
A7
D
D.S. al Coda
pup grows up! And we'll fight like twen - ty ar - mies and we won't give up! A
CODA
G
Em7
D/A
A7
D
flea can bite the bot - tom of the Pope in Rome!

I DON'T WANT TO LIVE ON THE MOON
from the Television Series *Sesame Street*

Words and Music by
Jeff Moss

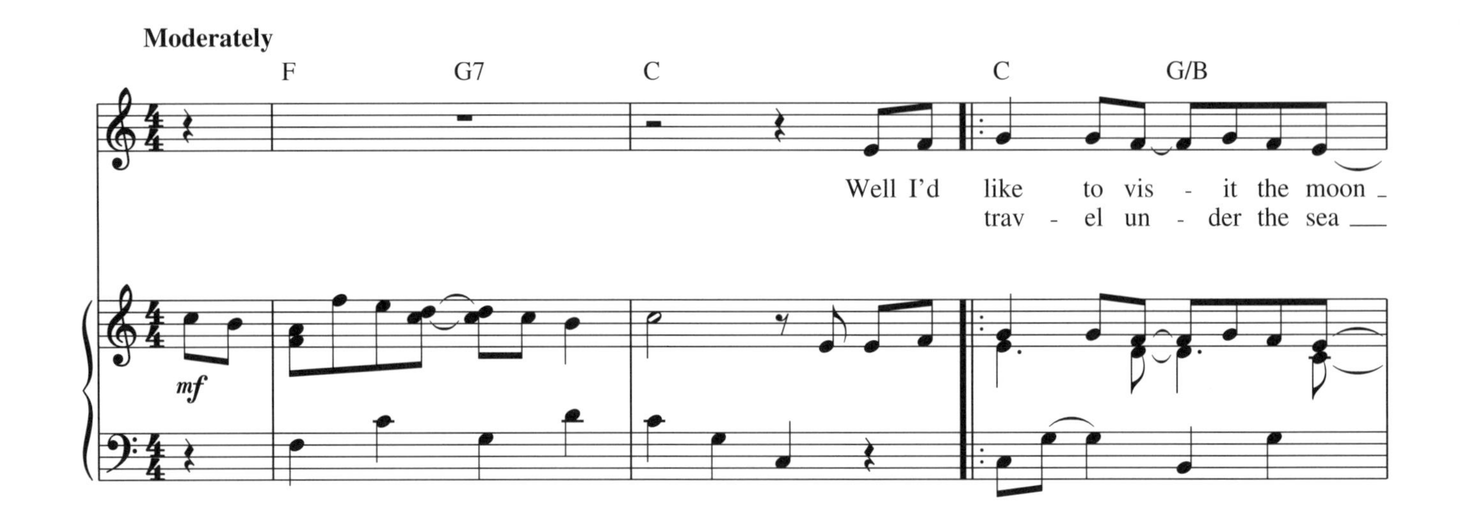

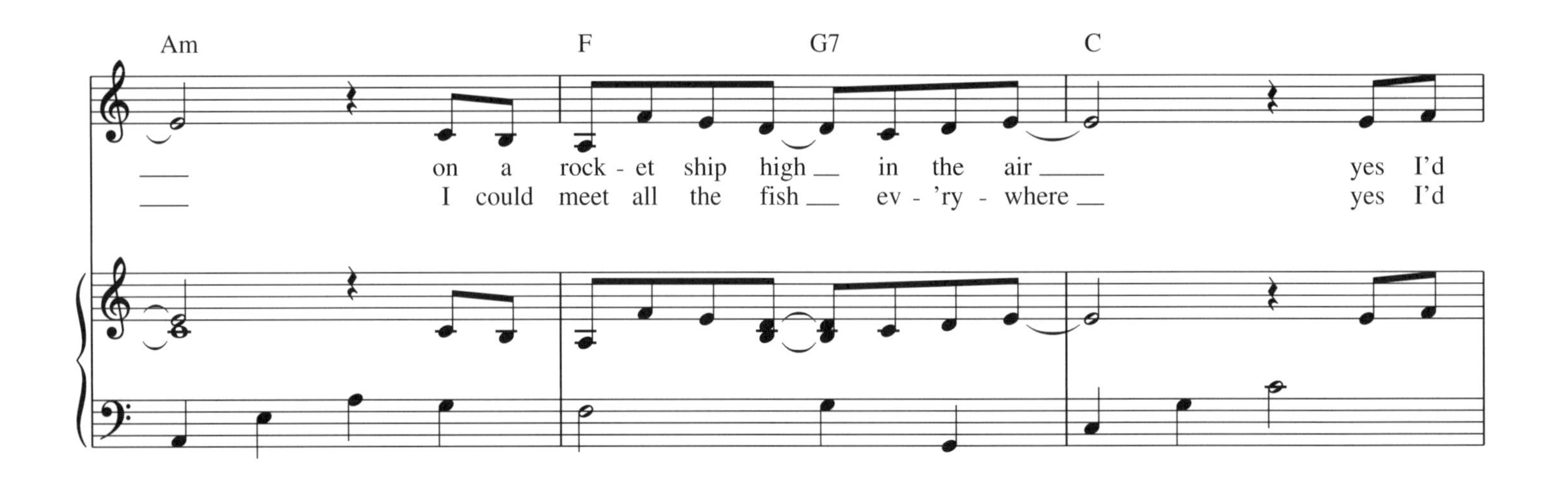

C
F
C/E
Dm7
G7
C
there. Though I'd like to look down at the earth from a - bove soon I'd
there. I might stay for a day there if I had my wish. But there's
F
C/E
Dm7
G7
C
F
C/E
miss all the plac - es and peo - ple I love so al - though I might like it for
not much to do when your friends are all fish and an oy - ster and clam are - n't
E7/G♯
Am
F
G7
1
C
one af - ter - noon I don't want to live on the moon. I'd like to
real fam - i - ly so I don't want to live in the
2
C
F
C/E
Dm7
G7
C
sea. I'd like to vis - it the jun - gle hear the li - on roar

F C/E Dm7 G7 C F C/E
go back in time _ and meet a di - no - saur. _ There's so man - y strange _ plac - es
E7/G♯ Am F G7 C
I'd like to be ___ but none of them per - ma - nent - ly. So if
G/B Am F G7
I should vis - it the moon _ well I'll dance on a moon - beam and then _
C G/B Am
___ I will make a wish _ on a star ___ and I'll

F G7 C F C/E
wish I was home once a - gain. Though I'd like to look down at the earth
Dm7 G7 C F C Dm7 G7 C
from a - bove soon I'd miss all the plac - es and peo - ple I love so al -
F C/E E7/G♯ Am F G7 C
though I may go I'll be com-ing home soon 'cause I don't want to live on the moon. No I
F G7sus G7 C
don't want to live on the moon.

I WON'T GROW UP

from *Peter Pan*

Lyric by Carolyn Leigh
Music by Mark Charlap

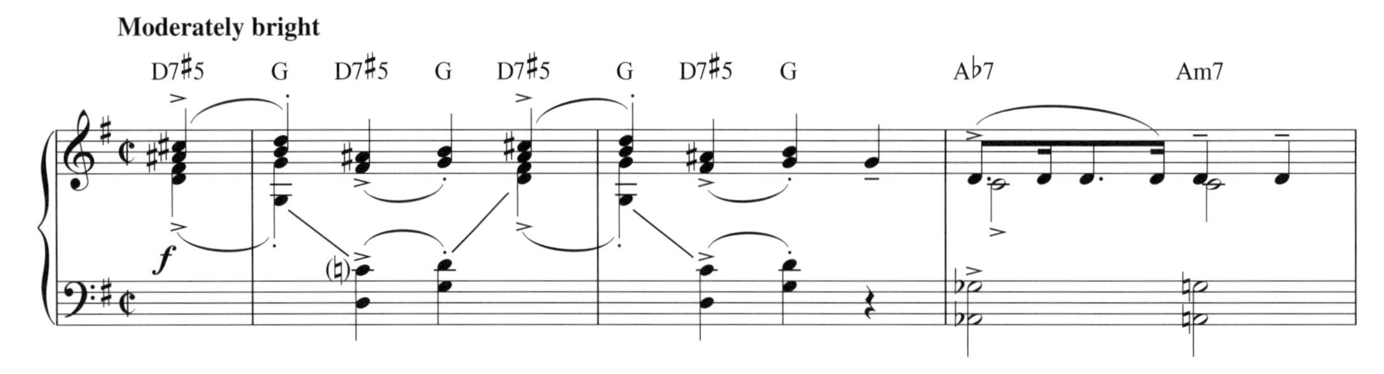

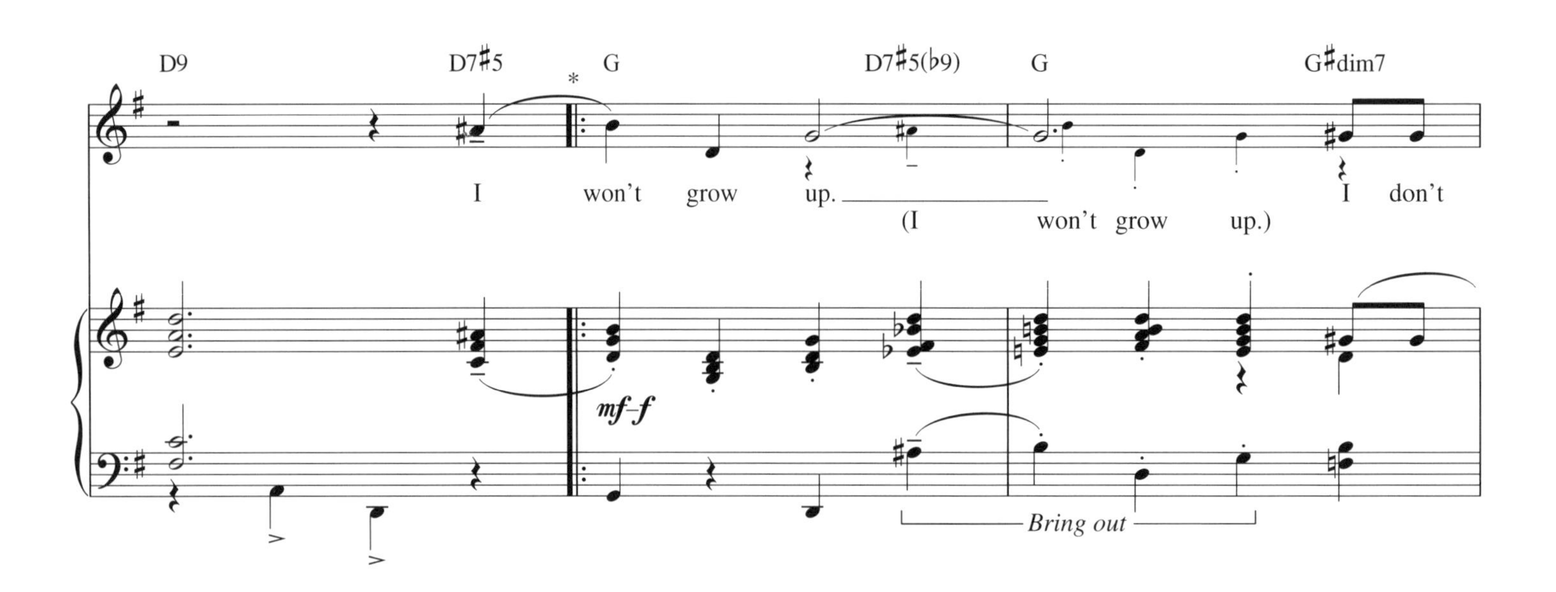

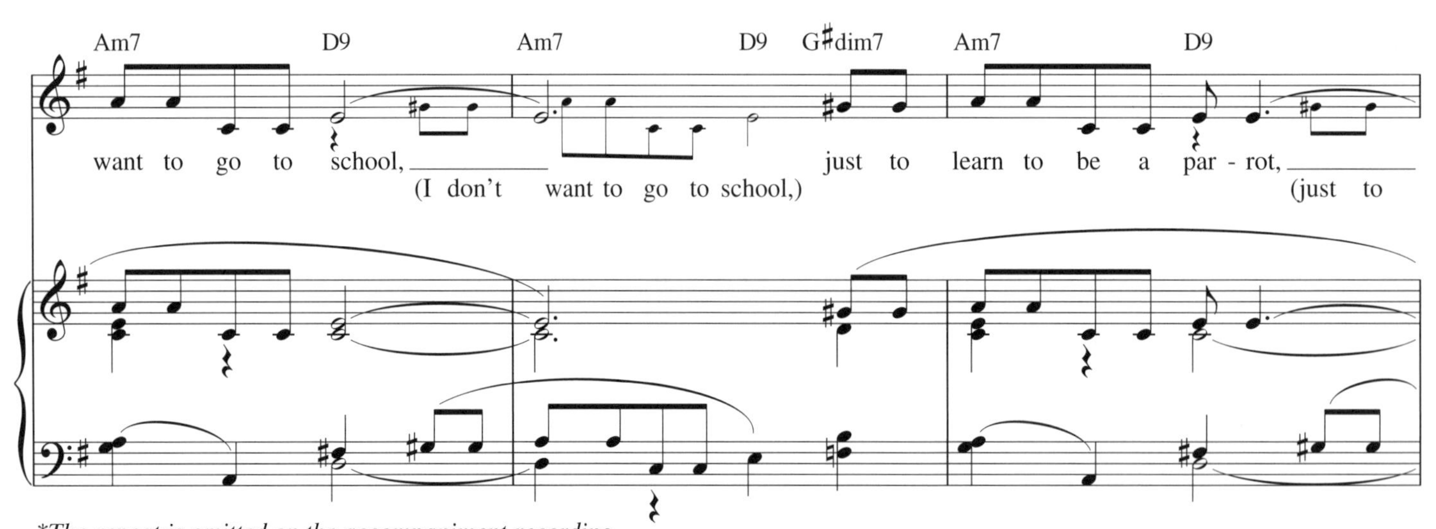

*The repeat is omitted on the accompaniment recording.
This song is performed by The Lost Boys in the show, adapted here as a solo.*

Am7 D9 D7♯5 G D7♯5(♭9) G6 G7
and re - cite a sil - ly rule. If
learn to be a par - rot,) (and re - cite a sil - ly rule.)
Cmaj7 Cm6 Em7 B7♭9 E E7♭9
grow - ing up means it would be be - neath my dig - ni - ty to climb a tree, I'll
A9 Am7♭5 D7 D7♭9 G6 D7
nev - er grow up, nev - er grow up, nev - er grow up, not me! Not
G6 D7♭9 G6 D7 G6 D7♯5 G D7♯5(♭9)
I! Not me! Not me! I won't grow up. (I
8va
15ma
Bring

G G♯dim7 Am7 D9 Am7 D9 G♯dim7
I don't want to wear a tie and a
won't grow up.) (I don't want to wear a tie)
out
Am7 D9 Am7 D9 D7♯5 G D7♭9 G D7♯5(♭9)
se - ri - ous ex - pres - sion in the mid - dle of Ju - ly.
(and a se - ri - ous ex - pres - sion) (in the
G6 G7 Cmaj7 Cm6
And if it means I must pre - pare to
mid - dle of Ju - ly.)
Em7 B7♭9 E7 E7♭9 A9
shoul - der bur - dens with a wor - ried air, I'll nev - er grow up, nev - er

Am7♭5
D7
D7♭9
G6
D7
G6
D7♭9
grow up, nev - er grow up, so there! Not I! Not
8va
15ma
G6
D7
G6
G7
F♯dim7
G7
C
me! So there! Nev - er gon - na be a man,
(15ma)
D7
D7♯5(♭9)
G
C
D7♯5(♭9)
G
I won't! Like to see some-bod - y try and make me.
B7♭9
Em
A7
D7sus
An - y - one who wants to try and make me turn in - to a man,

D9
D7♯5
G
D7♯5(♭9)
G
G♯dim7
catch me if you can. I won't grow up.
Not a
(I won't grow up.)
Bring out
Am7
D9
Am7
D9
G♯dim7
Am7
D9
pen - ny will I pinch.
I will nev - er grow a mus - tache
(Not a pen-ny will I pinch.)
(I will
Am7
D9
D7♯5
G
D7♭9
G
D7♯5(♭9)
G6
G
or a frac - tion of an inch.
'Cause
nev-er grow a mus-tache)
(or a frac-tion of an inch.)
Cmaj7
Cm6
Em7
B7♭9
grow - ing up is aw - full - er than all the aw - ful things that

E7 E7♭9 A9 Am7♭5
ev - er were. I'll nev - er grow up, nev - er grow up, nev - er grow
D7 D7♭9 1 G6 D7 G6 D7♭9
up, no sir! Not I! Not
8va
G6 D7 G6 D7♯9 2 G6 Dmaj7♯5 G Dmaj7♯5
me! No sir! I sir, not I, not
(8va) 15ma
G Dmaj7♯5 G D7♭5 G
me, I won't, no sir!
ff

I'M LATE

from Walt Disney's *Alice in Wonderland*

Words by Bob Hilliard
Music by Sammy Fain

A7/C♯
Dm
Gm/D
Dm
F7
B♭/F
whis - kers took me too much time to shave. I run and then I hop, hop, hop; I
mf
F7
B♭
A7
Dm
wish that I could fly. There's dan - ger if I dare to stop and
r.h.
C7
F7
B♭m
here's the rea - son why (you see) I'm o - ver - due; I'm in a rab - bit
C7
B♭
F7
B♭
E♭
B♭
B♭6
stew. Can't e - ven say good - bye, hel - lo, I'm late, I'm late, I'm late.

I'VE GOT NO STRINGS

from Walt Disney's *Pinocchio*

Words by Ned Washington
Music by Leigh Harline

18
C7
C
C7(♯5)
F6
C7
me, not me; you see, I've got no strings so I have fun, I'm
mf
23
F6
C7
Gm7sus4
B♭/C A7/C♯
not tied up to an - y one! How I love my li - ber - ty, there are no strings on
28
Dm
Csus4(9)
C7
D♭7
me! There are no strings! I said no strings! I've
f
subito p
f
subito p
33
Gm7sus4
C
F
got no strings on me!
cresc.
sfz

IN MY OWN LITTLE CORNER

from *Cinderella*

Lyrics by Oscar Hammerstein II
Music by Richard Rodgers

* *The repeat is omitted on the accompaniment recording.*

E♭ E♭6 E♭ C7
cor - ner, in my own lit - tle chair, I can be what -
F C7 F
ev - er I want to be. On the wing of my
E♭ E♭6 E♭ C7
fan - cy I can fly an - y - where And the world will
F D
o - pen its arms to me. I'm a young Nor - we - gian
legato

A7sus A7 F♯m D Bm F♯7
prin - cess or a milk - maid, I'm the great - est pri - ma don - na in Mi -
Bm Gm(maj7) Gm D/A A7sus A7
lan. I'm an heir - ess who has al - ways had her
D A/E E7
silk made By her own flock of silk - worms in Ja -
A Gm7 C7 F
pan. I'm a girl men go mad for, love's a
mp

E♭
E♭6
E♭
C7
3
game I can play with a cool and con - fi - dent kind of
F7
B♭
B♭m/D♭
air, Just as long as I stay in my own lit - tle
cresc.
mf
F/C
B♭(add9)
F/C
Gm/C
C7
cor - ner, All a - lone in my own lit - tle
1
2
F
Gm7
C7
F
chair. In my chair.
mp
mf

JOIN THE CIRCUS

from *Barnum*

Music by Cy Coleman
Lyrics by Michael Stewart
Arranged by Michael Dansicker

This song is an ensemble number in the show, adapted here as a solo.

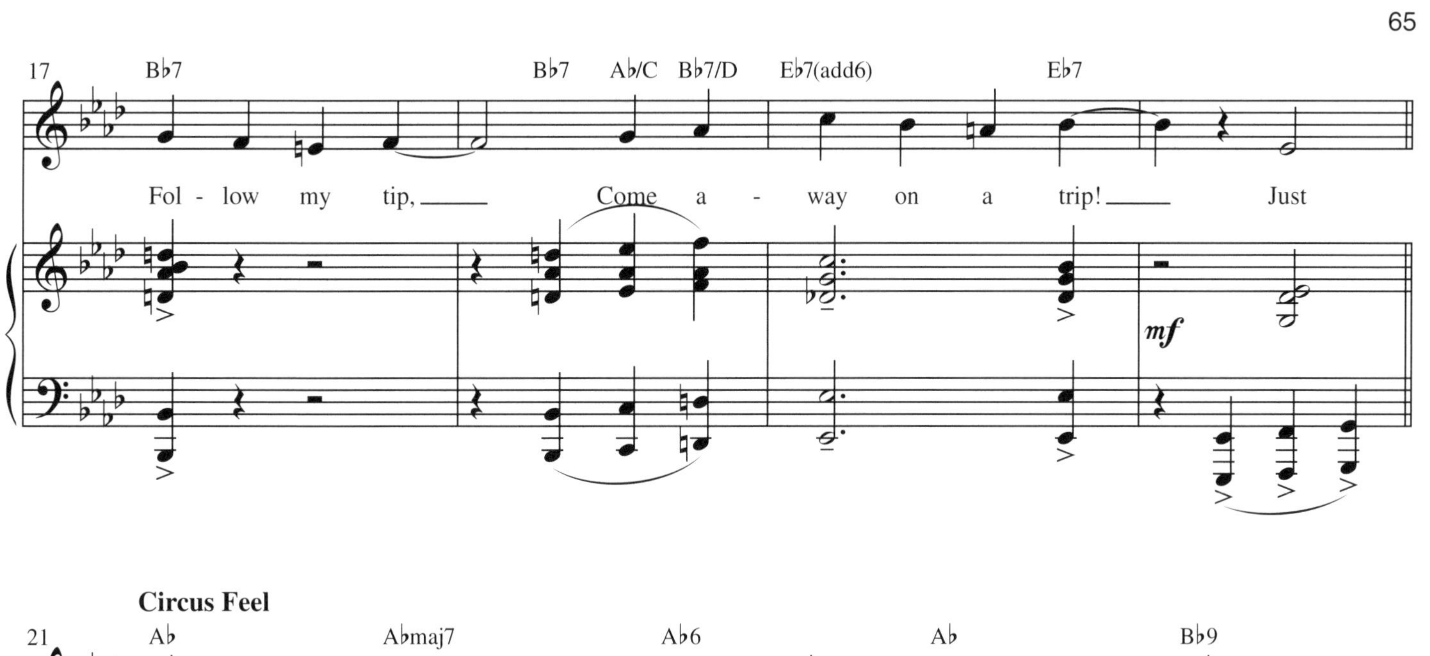
17
B♭7
B♭7 A♭/C B♭7/D
E♭7(add6)
E♭7
Fol - low my tip, Come a - way on a trip! Just
mf

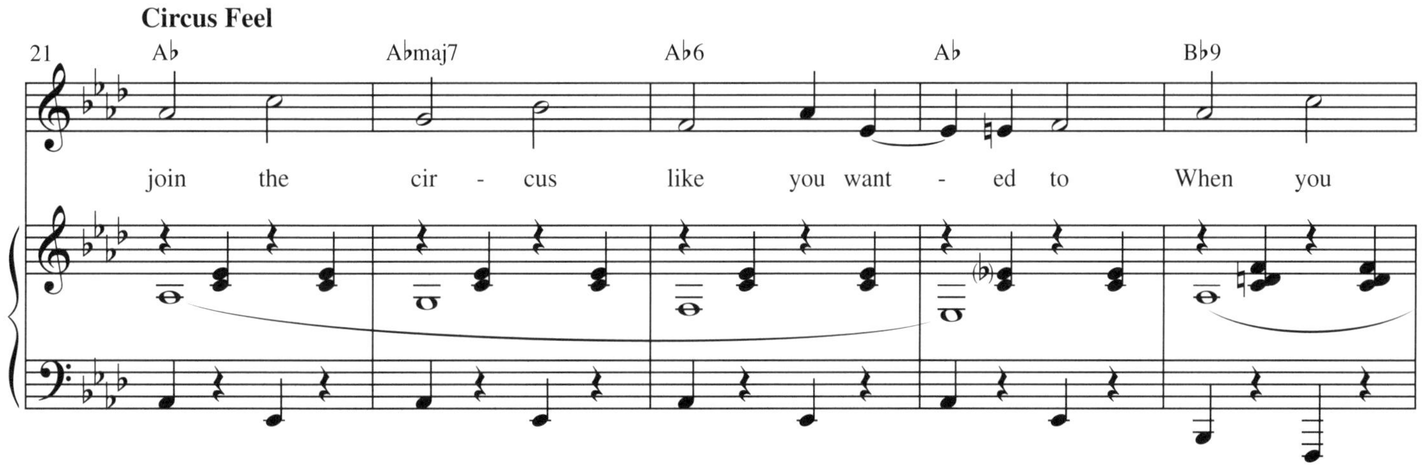
Circus Feel
21
A♭
A♭maj7
A♭6
A♭
B♭9
join the cir - cus like you want - ed to When you

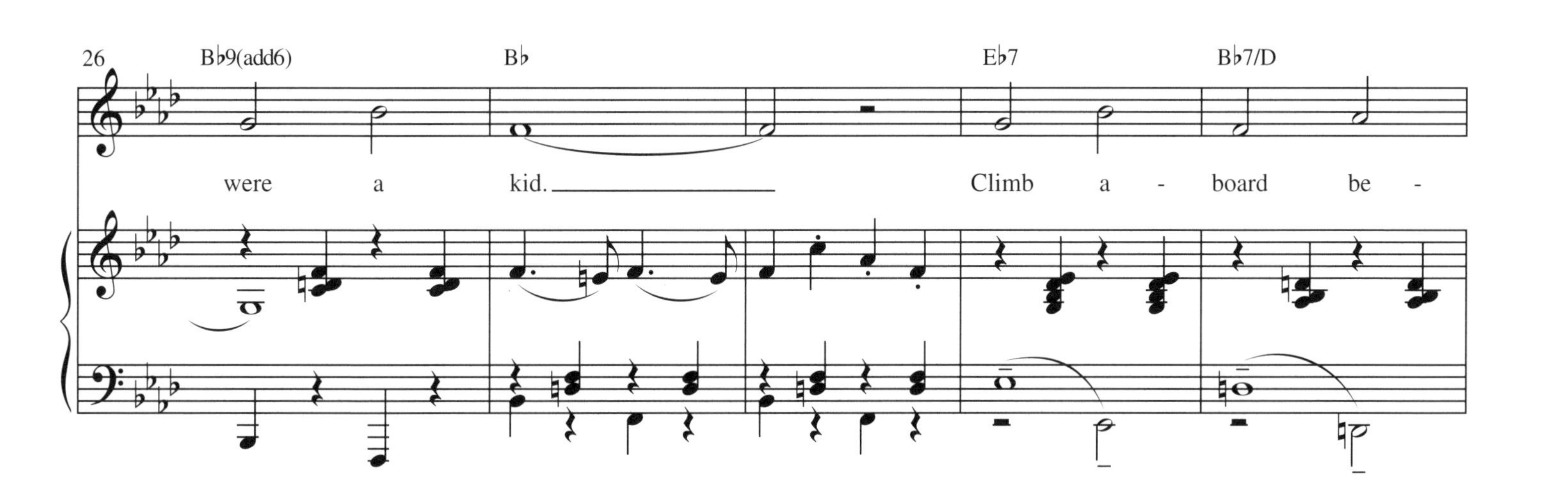
26
B♭9(add6)
B♭
E♭7
B♭7/D
were a kid. Climb a - board be -

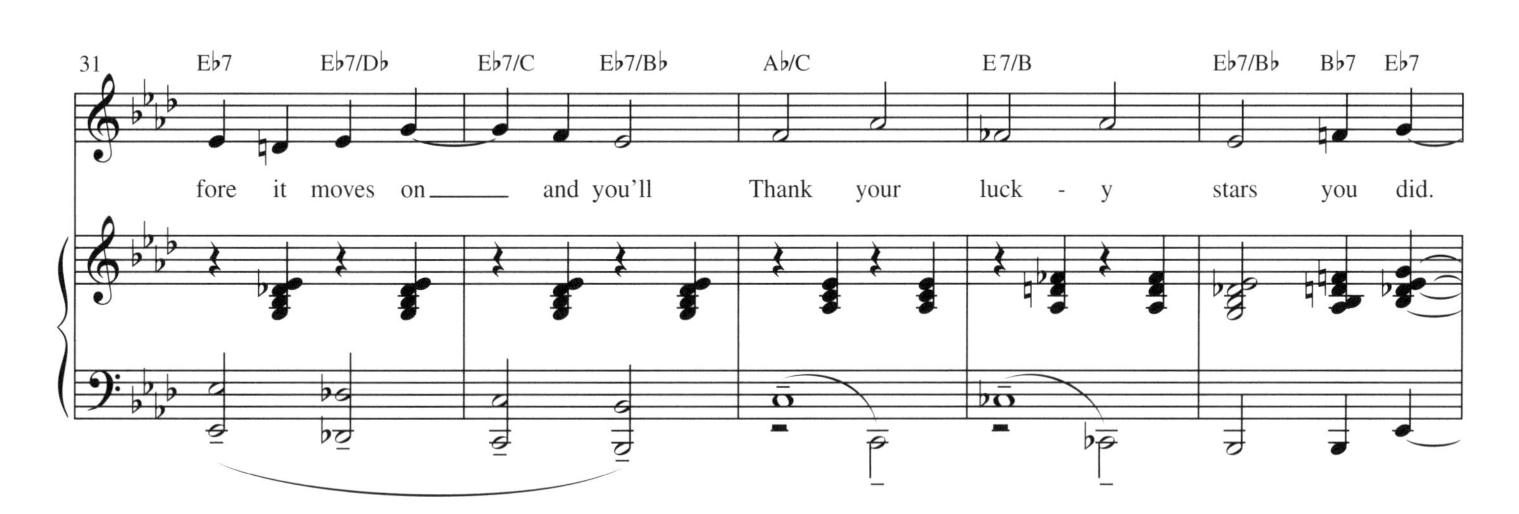
31
E♭7 E♭7/D♭
E♭7/C E♭7/B♭
A♭/C
E 7/B
E♭7/B♭ B♭7 E♭7
fore it moves on and you'll Thank your luck - y stars you did.

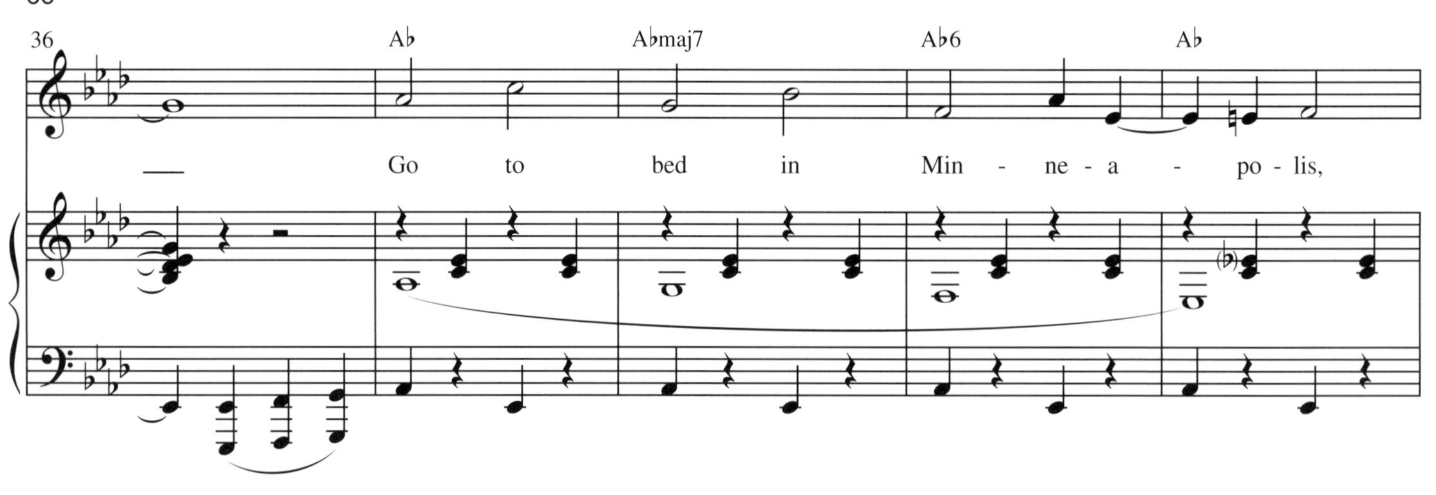
36
A♭
A♭maj7
A♭6
A♭
Go to bed in Min - ne - a - po - lis,

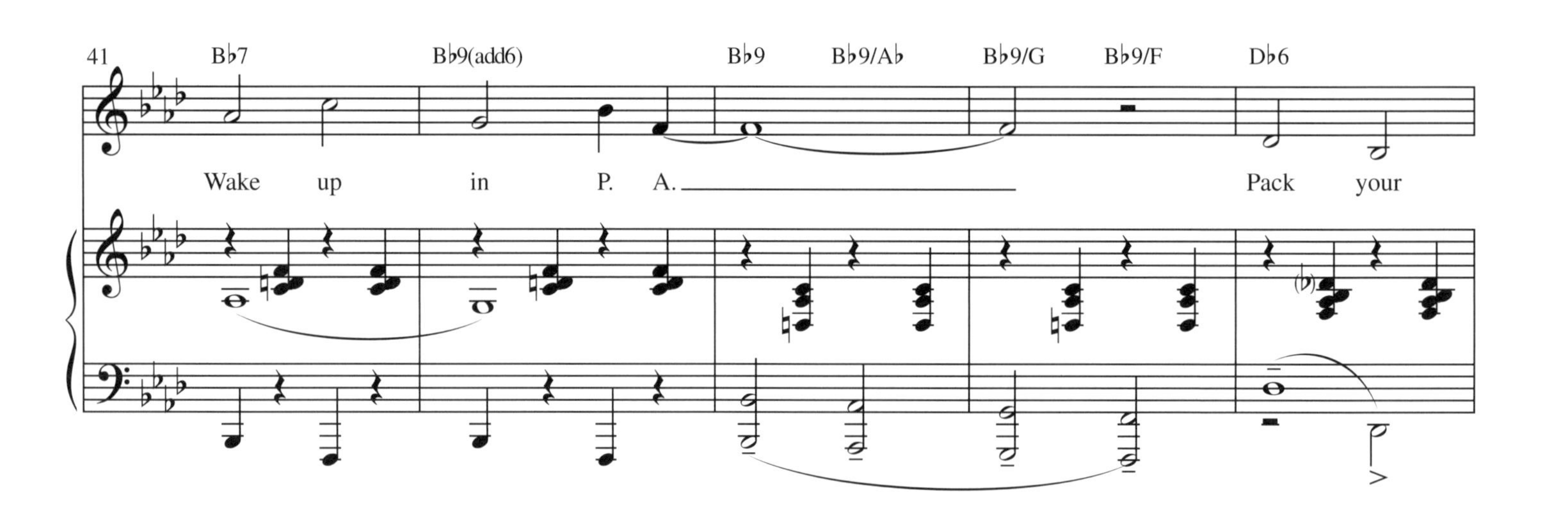
41
B♭7
B♭9(add6)
B♭9
B♭9/A♭
B♭9/G
B♭9/F
D♭6
Wake up in P. A.
Pack your

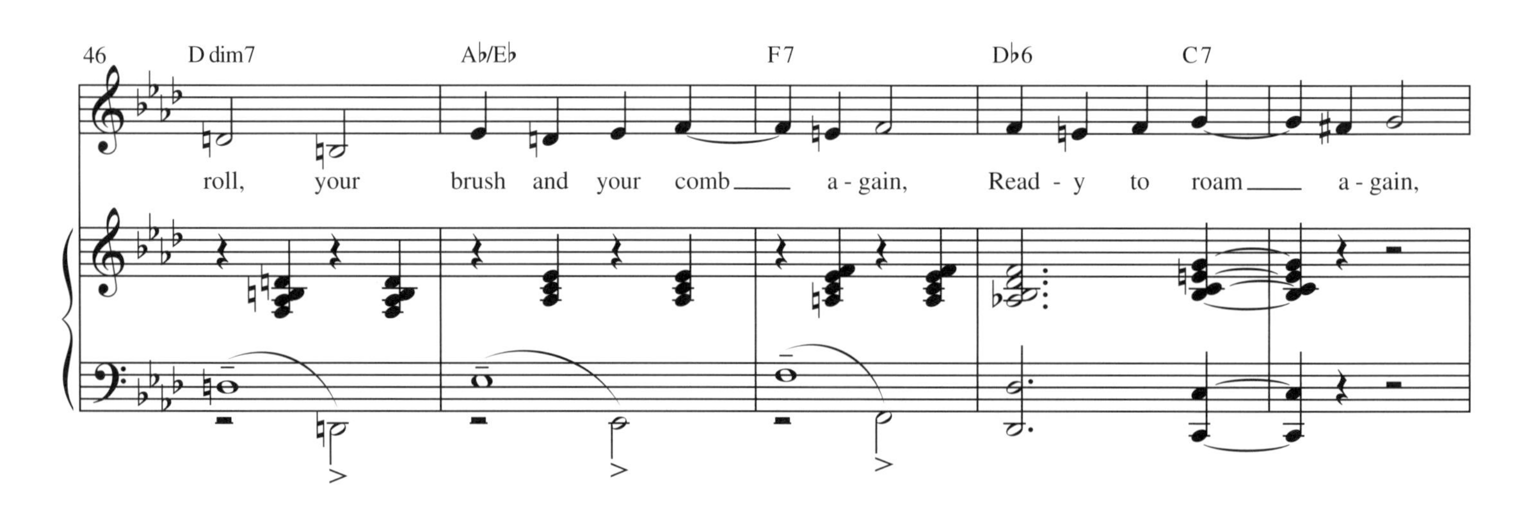
46
D dim7
A♭/E♭
F7
D♭6
C7
roll, your brush and your comb a - gain, Read - y to roam a - gain,

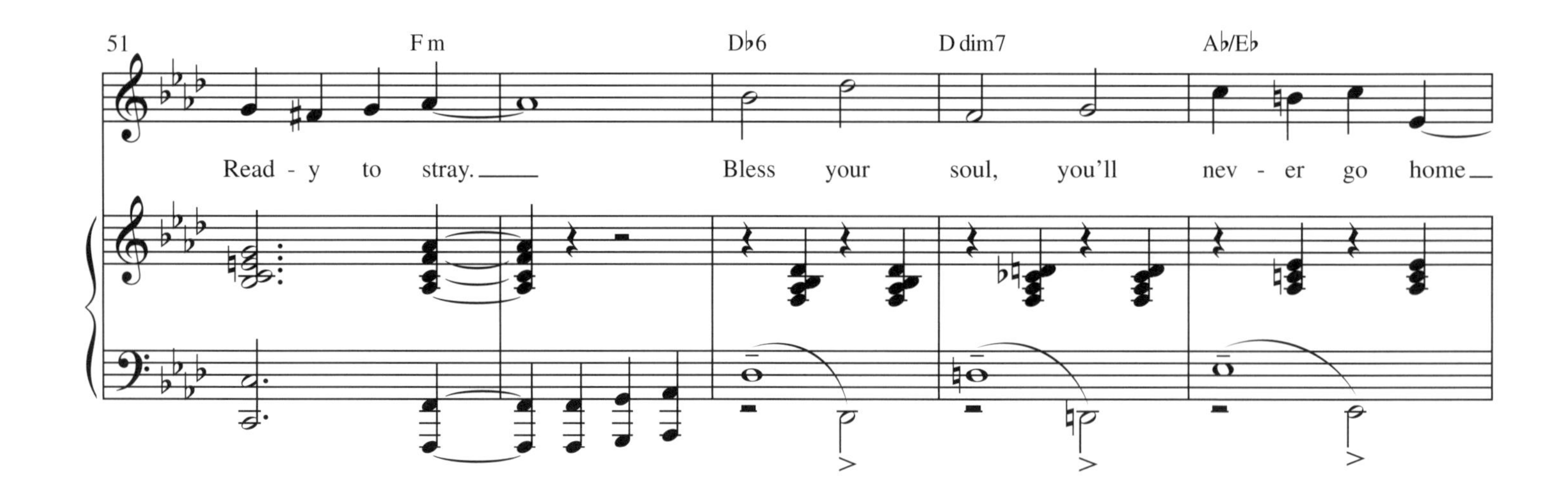
51
F m
D♭6
D dim7
A♭/E♭
Read - y to stray.
Bless your soul, you'll nev - er go home

56
F7
B♭7
B♭9
E♭7
— a - gain,
When the cir - cus comes your
sfz
sfz
61
C7
F7
way.
65
B♭7
E♭7
Run
a -
69
A♭
way!
sfz
sfz
sfz

MY BEST GIRL (MY BEST BEAU)

Music and Lyric by Jerry Herman
Arranged by Michael Dansicker

* This may be used as a substitute throughout.
This song is performed by Patrick and Mame Dennis in the show, adapted here as a solo.

21
Bm7 E7(♭5) E7 A F♯m
oth - er girl comes a - long, It won't take her long to
25
B9 G♯m C♯7 F♯m
see, That I'll still be found just
29
Bm7(♭5) F+/C♯ Dm A+/E Esus E7
hang - in' a - round My best
33
A F7 E♭/F F7 B♭ Dm Cm7
girl. And if some - day an - oth - er girl comes a -
mf

38
F7(♭5)
F7
B♭
Gm
C9
Am
D7
long, It won't take her long to see, That
43
Gm
Cm7(♭5)
G♭+/D
E♭m
B♭+/F
I'll still be found just hang-in' a - round MY
48
Fsus4
F7
Gm
Cm7
Gm/D
Cm
B♭+/F
Fsus4
F7
BEST GIRL! MY BEST
rall.
mp
poco rit.
53
B♭
Dm
Cm7
F7
B♭
GIRL.
a tempo
rall.

PUT ON A HAPPY FACE

from *Bye Bye Birdie*

Lyric by Lee Adams
Music by Charles Strouse

G7 C7 F7 B♭7 E♭maj7 E♭7 E♭6
mask of trag - e - dy, it's not your style;
A♭maj7 D7 G7 C7 F13 B♭13
You'll look so good that you'll be glad ya' de - cid - ed to smile!
B♭9 E♭ E♭6 Gm7(add11) C7
Pick out a pleas - ant out - look,
Fm7 B♭9 Fm7 B♭9 E♭ E♭6
stick out that no - ble chin; Wipe off that "full of

Gm7(add11)
C7
Fm7
B♭9
B♭m7
E♭7
doubt" look,
slap on a hap - py grin!
And
A♭maj7
Dm7♭5
E♭
Fm11
B♭7
G7♯5
G7
C9
spread sun - shine all o - ver the place,
just
F13
B♭11
B♭13
opt.
1
E♭9
E♭6
put on a hap - py face!
Fm7
B♭7
2
E♭
E♭7
Fm7
E♭
face!

REAL LIVE GIRL
from *Little Me*

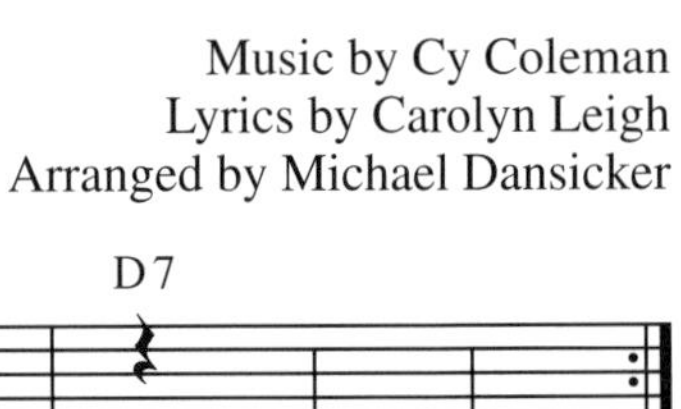

23
Gaug
Cmaj7
C6
F7(♯11)
F7
fec - tion - ate squeeze
Fogs up my gog - gles and buck - les my knees.
29
G/B
B♭dim7
Am7
D7
Baug
B
I'm sim - ply drowned in the sight and the sound and the scent and the
35
Eaug7
E7
A7sus4/E
A7
Am9
feel of a real live
40
D7
G
E♭7
girl.

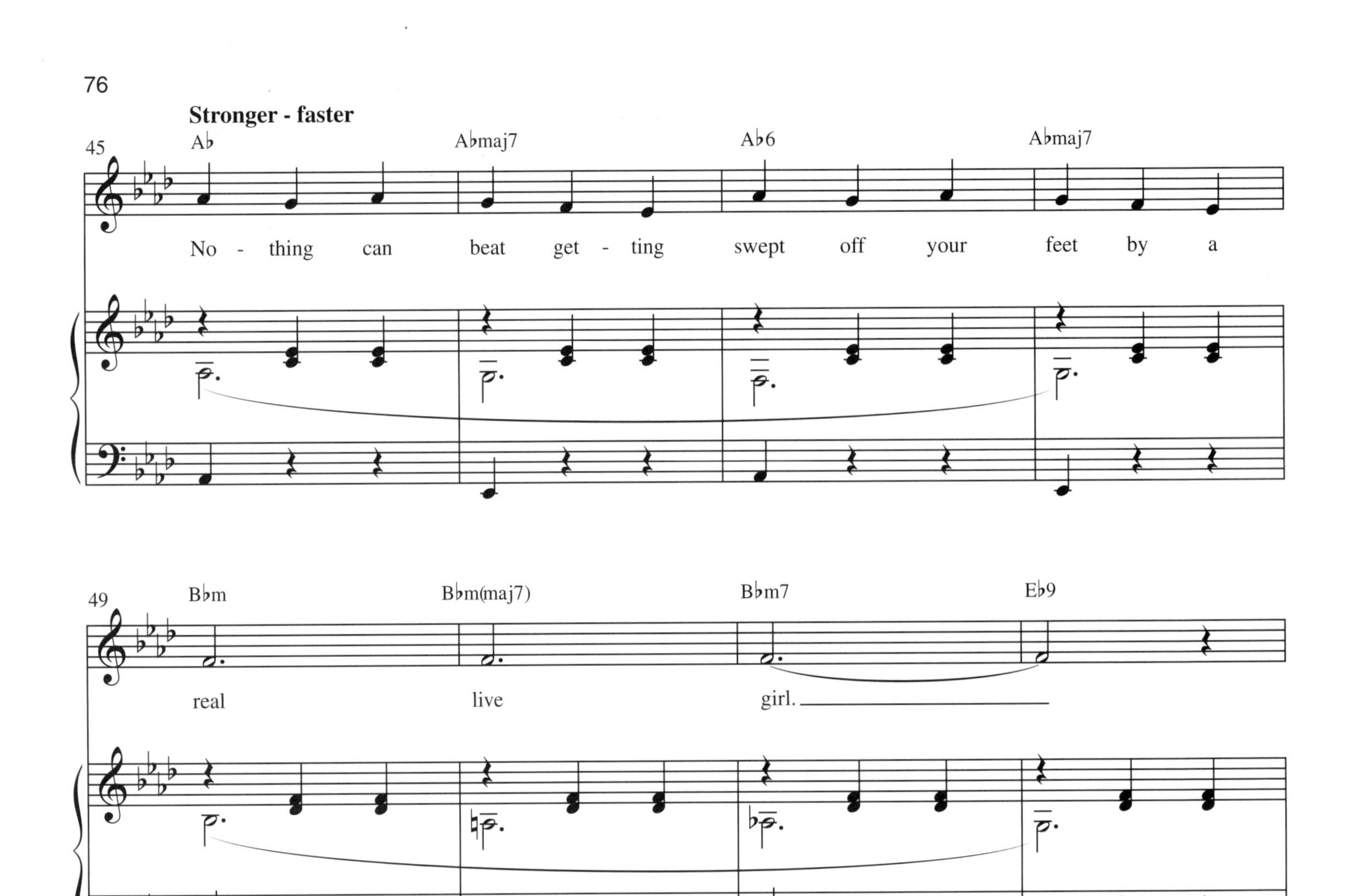
Stronger - faster
45
Ab Abmaj7 Ab6 Abmaj7
No - thing can beat get - ting swept off your feet by a
49
Bbm Bbm(maj7) Bbm7 Eb9
real live girl.

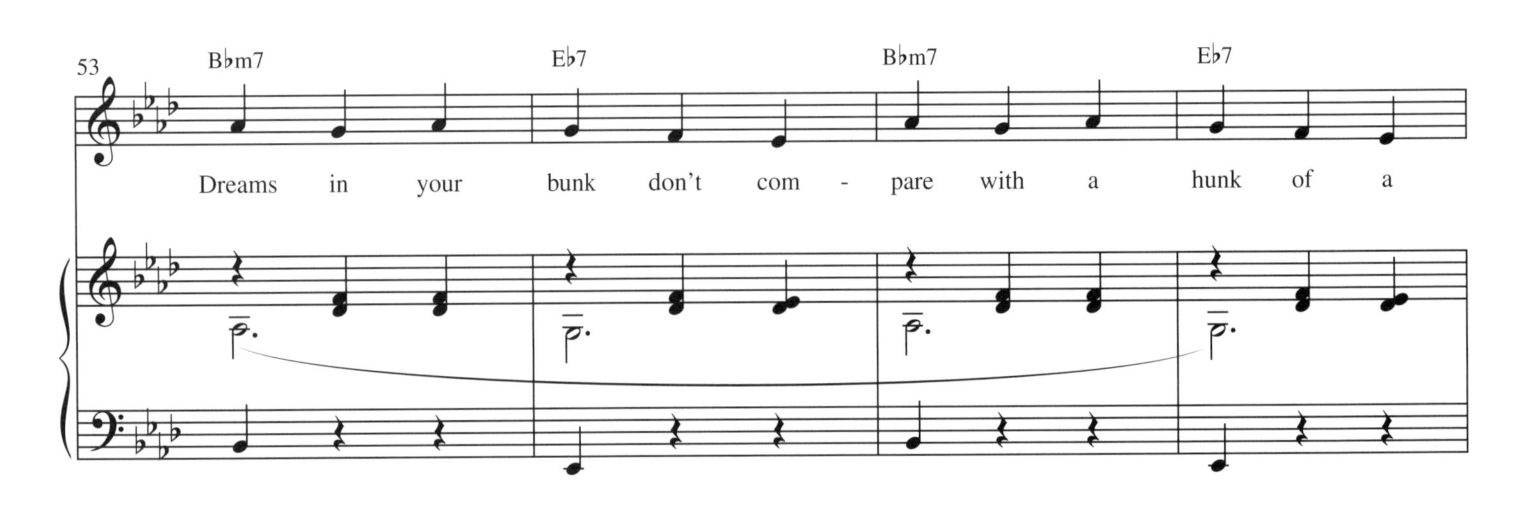
53
Bbm7 Eb7 Bbm7 Eb7
Dreams in your bunk don't com - pare with a hunk of a

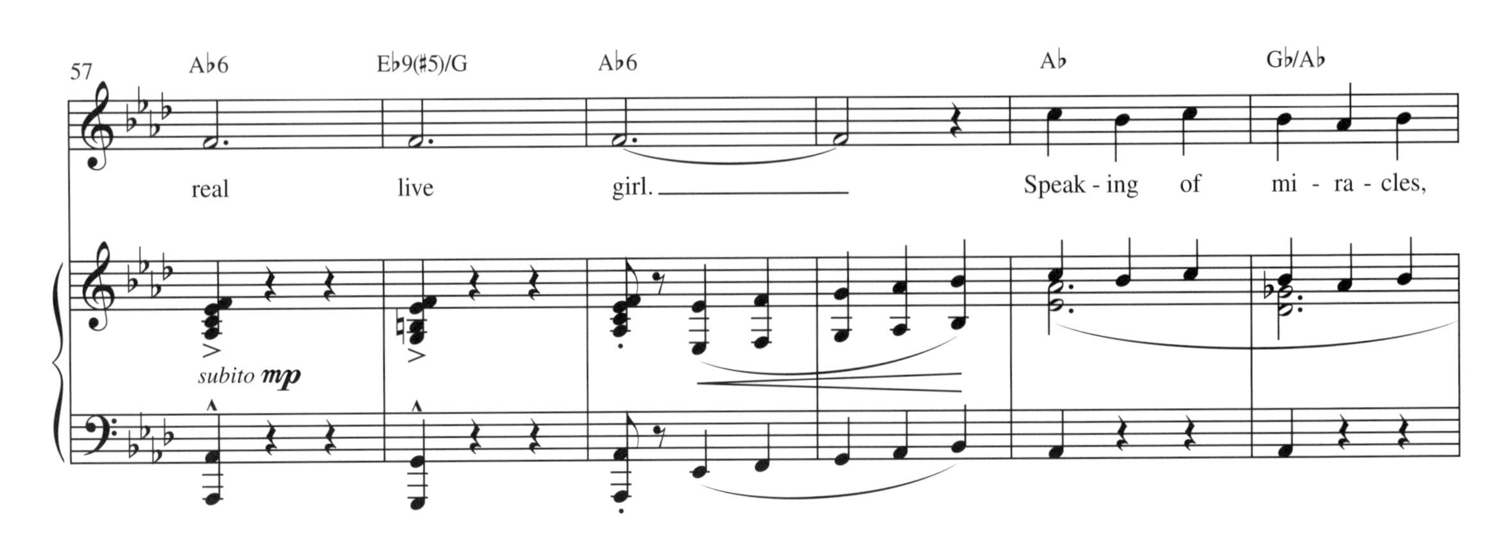
57
Ab6 Eb9(#5)/G Ab6 Ab Gb/Ab
real live girl. Speak - ing of mi - ra - cles,
subito mp

63
A♭aug
D♭maj7
D♭6
G♭7(♯11)
this must be it, Just when I start - ed to learn how to
68
G♭7
A♭/C
B dim7
B♭m7
E♭7
knit. I'm all in stitch - es from find - ing what rich - es a
73
C aug
C
F aug7
F7
B♭7sus4/F
B♭7
waltz can re - veal with a real
79
B♭m9
E♭7
A♭
live girl!
fff
Glissando

SING

from *Sesame Street*

Words and Music by
Joe Raposo

Am7
G
Gmaj7
G6
Dm7/G
song.
Make it
sim - ple
to
last your whole life
long.
G7
Dm7/G G7
Cmaj7
B7
Em7
A9
Don't
wor-ry that
it's
not
good
e - nough
for
an - y - one
else
to
hear.
Am7
G
D7
Sing!
Sing
a
song!
G
Gmaj7
Cmaj7
La
la
do
la
da,
La
da
la
do
la
da,
La
da
da
la
do
la
da.

G
Gmaj7
Cmaj7
1
2
La do la da, La da la la da, Lo da da la do lo da.
G
Gmaj7
Cmaj7
La la do la da, La da la do la da, La da da la do la da.
G
Gmaj7
Cmaj7
La la do la da, La da la do la da, La da da la do la da.
G
Gmaj7
Cmaj7
La la do la da, La da la do la da, La da da la do la da.

THE UGLY DUCKLING

from the Motion Picture *Hans Christian Andersen*

By Frank Loesser

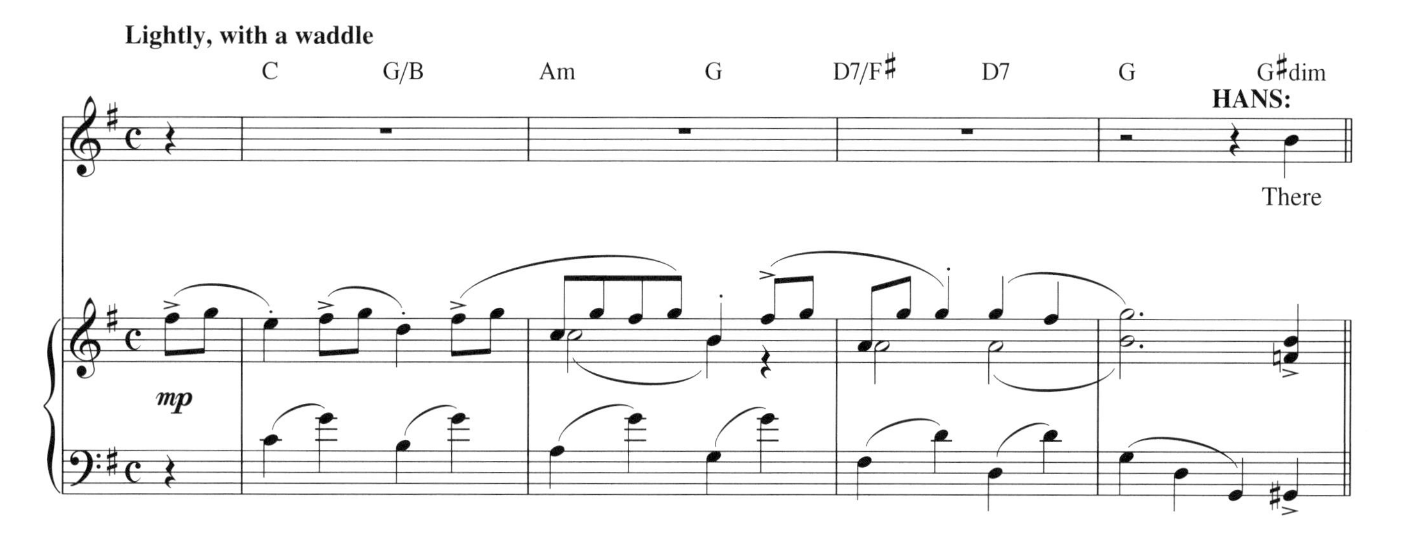

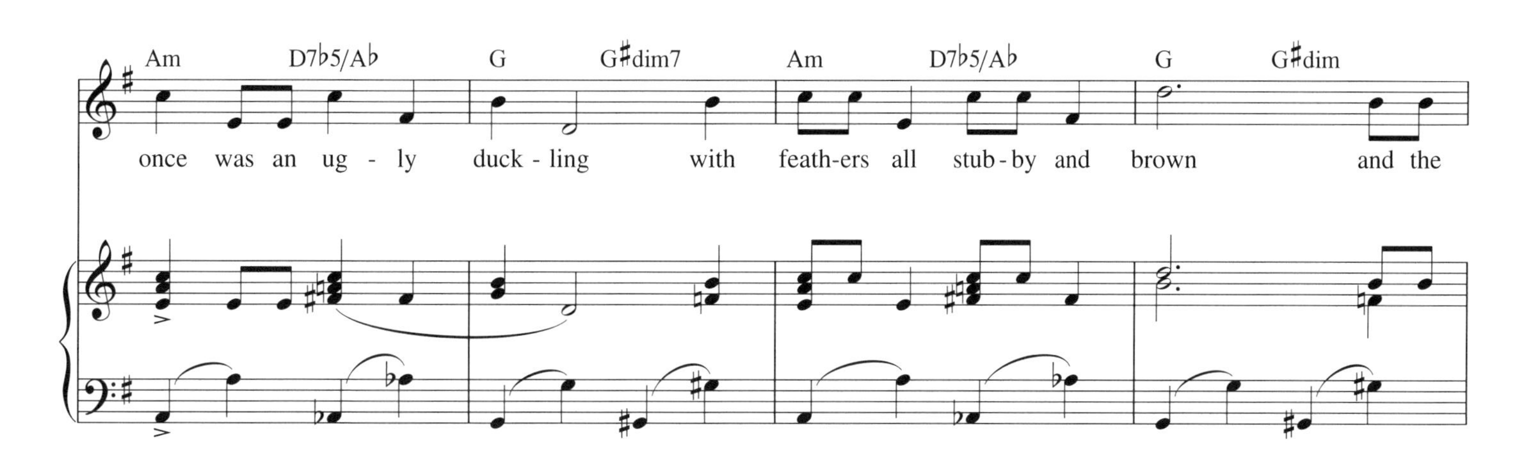

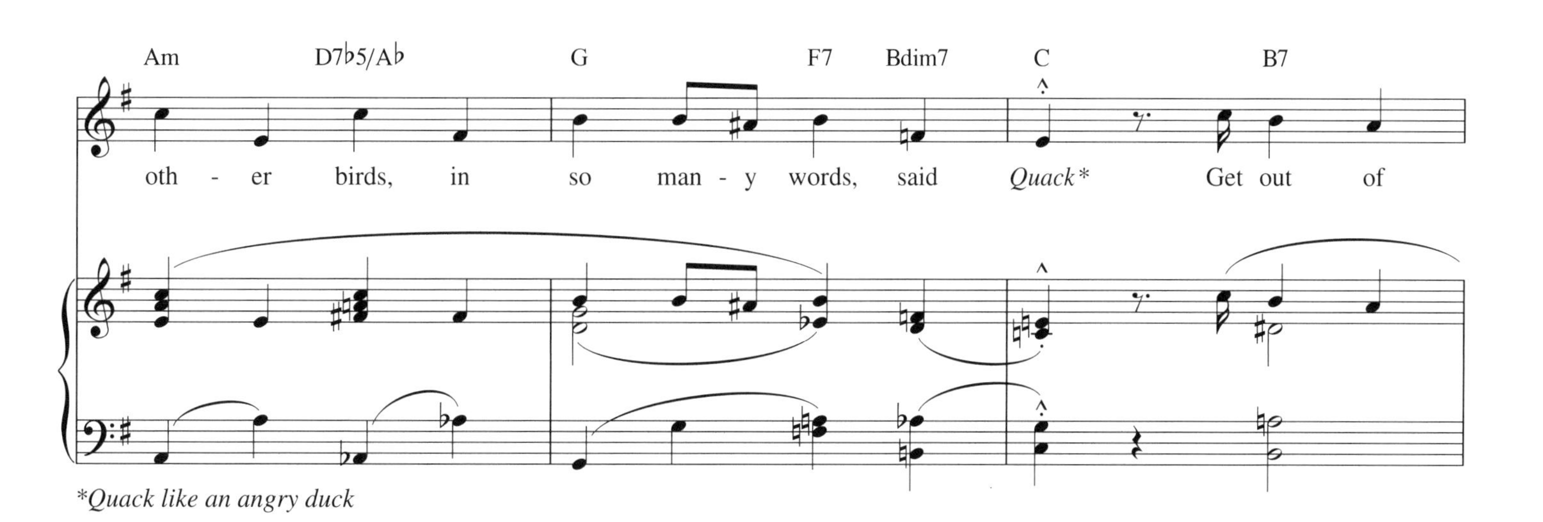

*Quack like an angry duck

Em G7 C Cm6 G/D Em Am D7sus D7
town. Quack get out, Quack Quack get out, Quack Quack get out of
G C G/B Am G
town. And he went with a quack and a wad - dle and a quack in a
D7/F♯ G C G/B Am G
opt.
flur - ry of Ei - der - down.
D7/F♯ D7 G G♯dim Am D7♭5/A♭ G G♯dim7
That poor lit - tle ug - ly duck - ling went

Am D7♭5/A♭ G G♯dim Am D7♭5/A♭ G F7 Bdim7
wan-der-ing far and near but at ev - 'ry place they said to his face now
C B7 Em G7 C Cm6 G/D Em
Quack get out of here Quack get out, Quack Quack get out, Quack
Am D7sus D7 G C G/B
Quack get out of here. And he went with a quack and a
Am G D7/F♯ G
opt.
wad - dle and a quack and a ver - y un - hap - py tear.

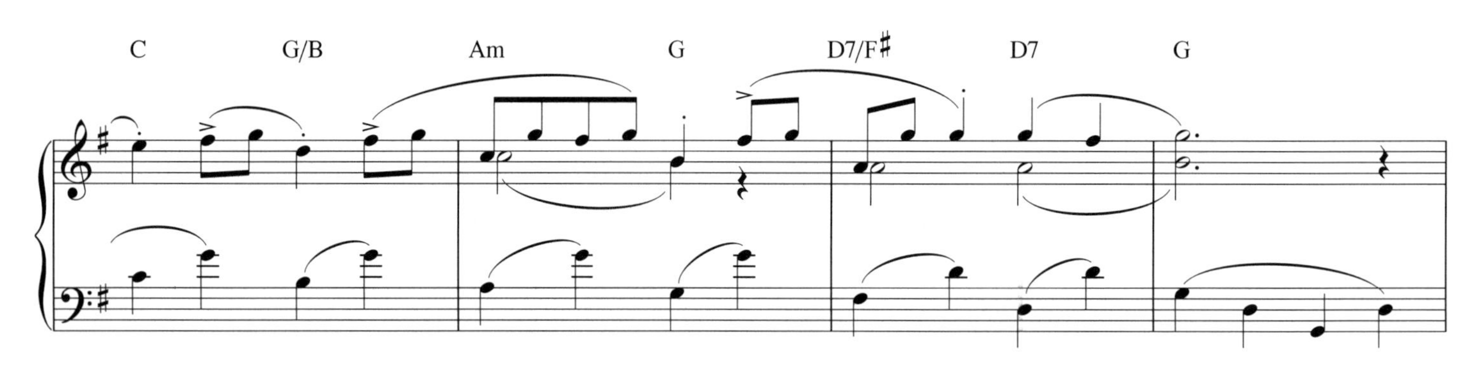
C
G/B
Am
G
D7/F♯
D7
G

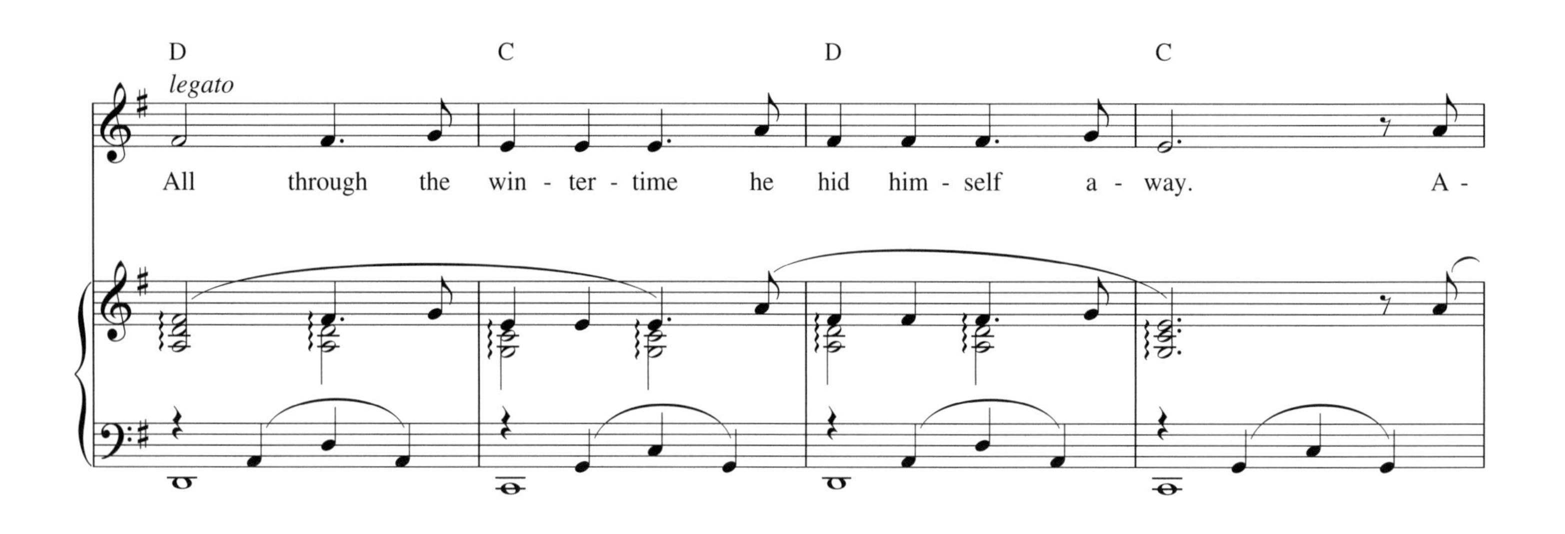
D
C
D
C
legato
All through the win - ter - time he hid him - self a - way. A -

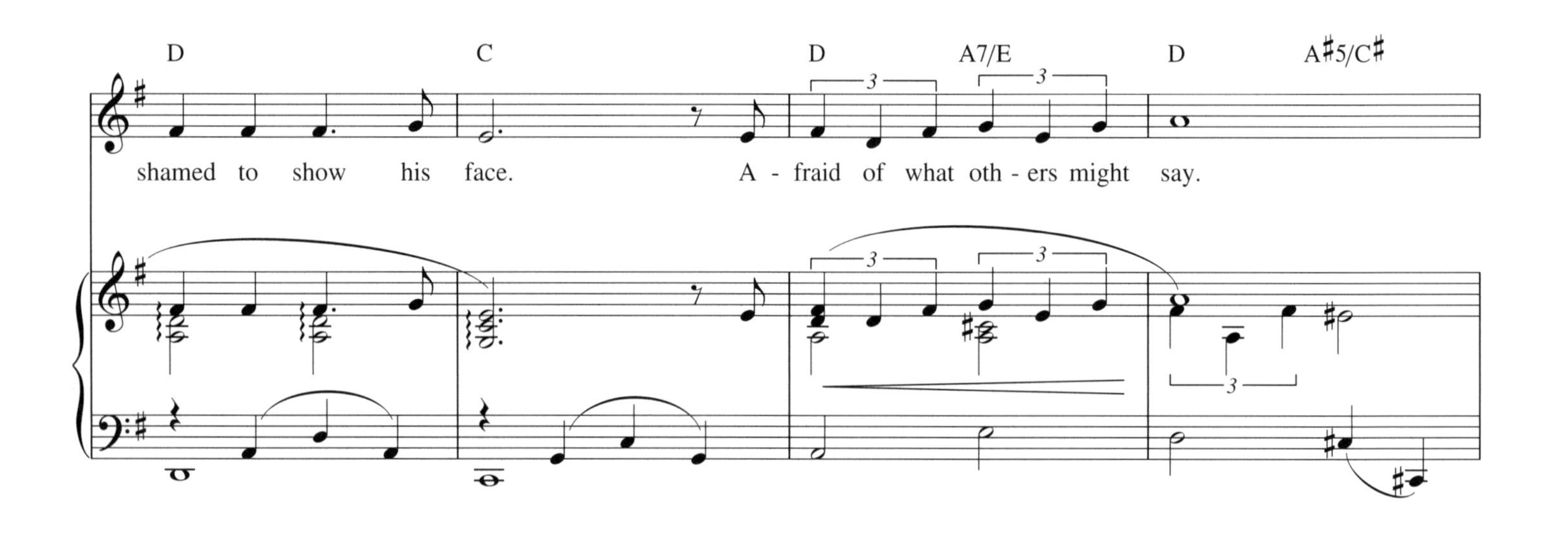
D
C
D
A7/E
D
A♯5/C♯
shamed to show his face. A - fraid of what oth - ers might say.

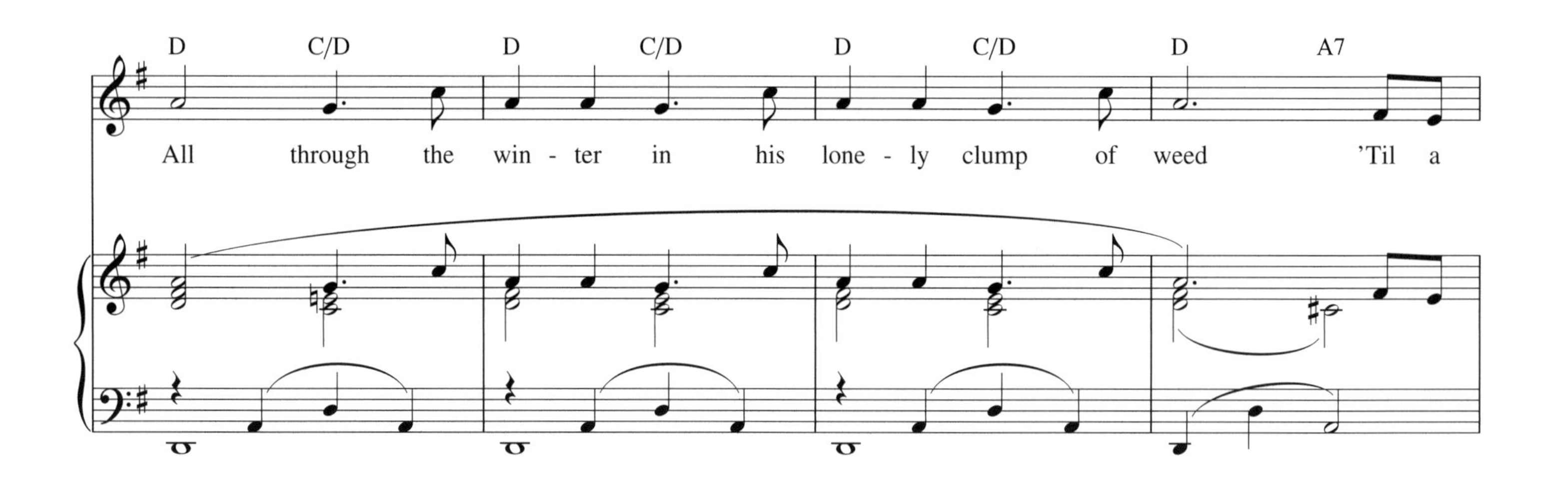
D
C/D
D
C/D
D
C/D
D
A7
All through the win - ter in his lone - ly clump of weed 'Til a

D
D7♭9
Am7♭5
flock of swans spied him there and ver - y soon a - greed: "You're a
f
D
Am7
D
ver - y fine swan in - deed!" (Spoken:) "Swan? Me a swan? Aw go
rit.
a tempo
sfz
D7♭9
on!" "You're a swan! Take a look at your - self in the
lake and you'll see!" And he looked and he saw, and he said, "Why, it's me! I

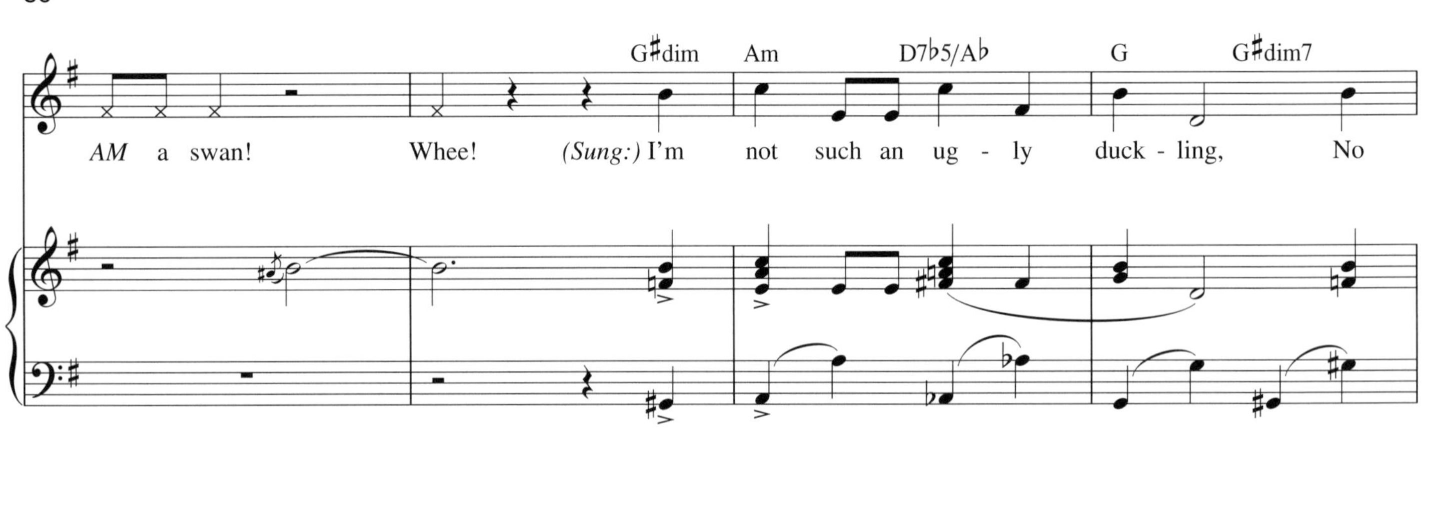

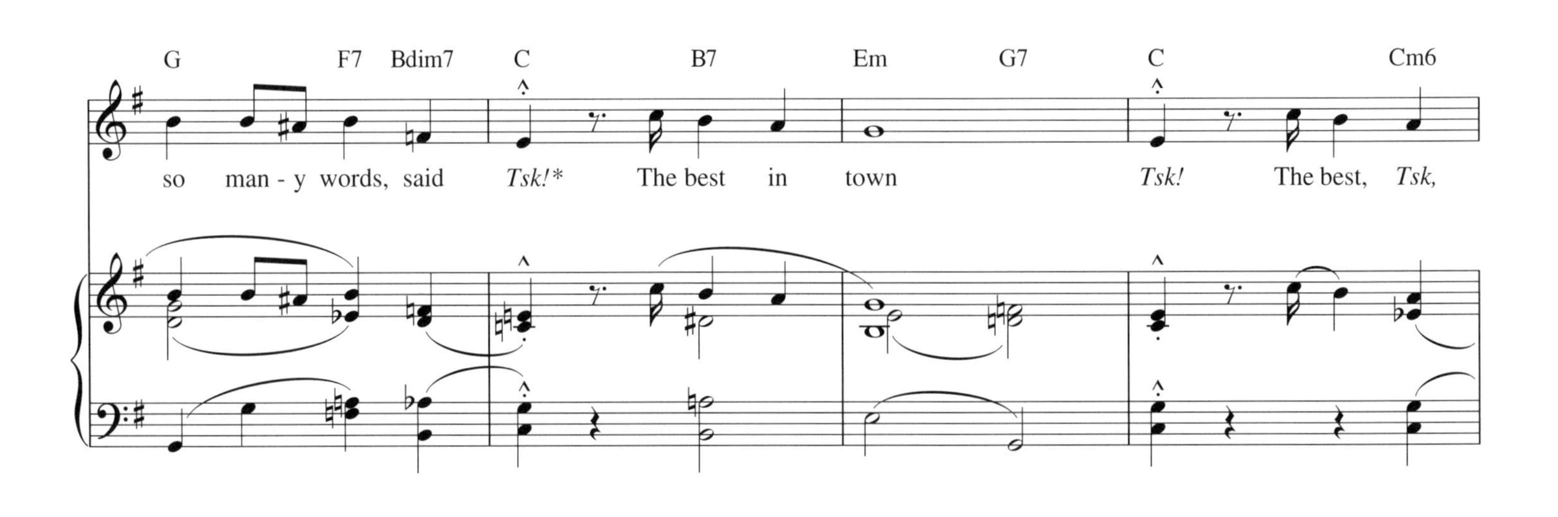

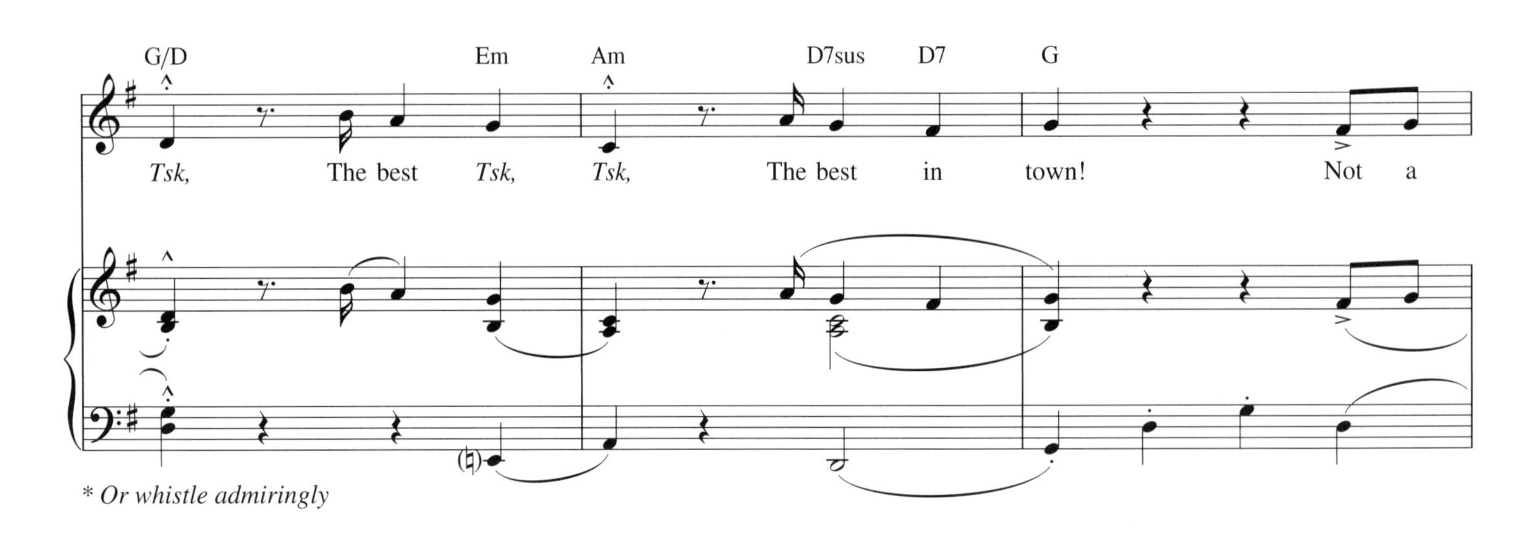

* Or whistle admiringly

C G/B Am G C G
quack, not a quack, not a wad - dle or a quack. But a glide and a whis - tle and a
A D G Am7 D7 G G♯dim7
ten.
snow - y white back and a head so no - ble and high! Say,
ten.
Am D7♭5/A♭ C D7 G Am/D G
who's an ug - ly duck - ling? Not I
(Whistle or hum)
C G/B Am G D7/F♯ D7 G
opt.
(Sung:) Not I!

SOMEONE'S WAITING FOR YOU

from Walt Disney's *The Rescuers*

Words by Carol Connors and Ayn Robbins
Music by Sammy Fain

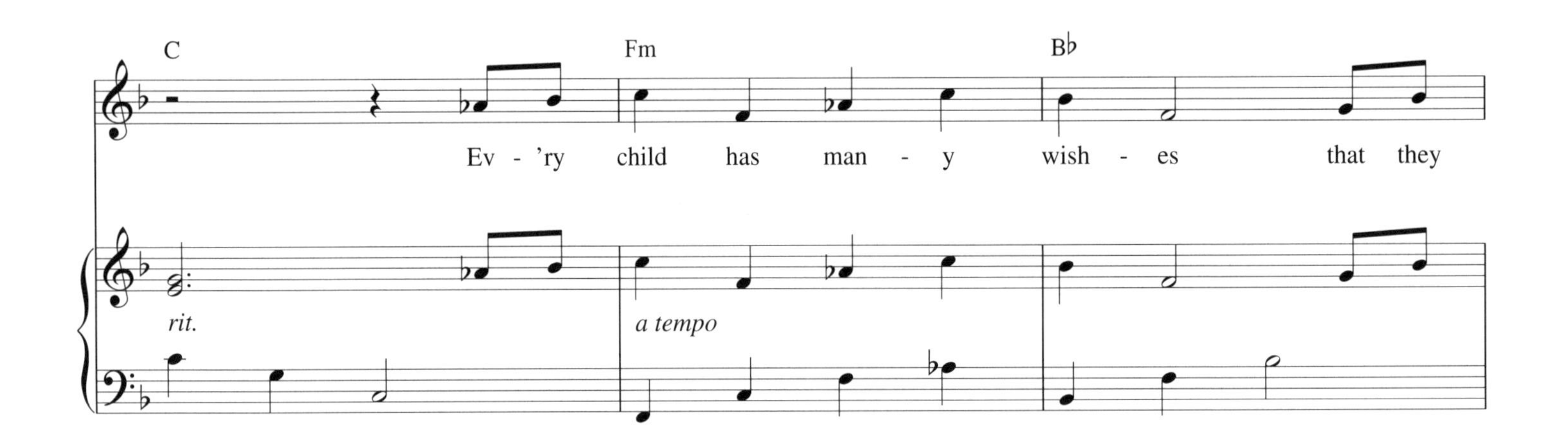

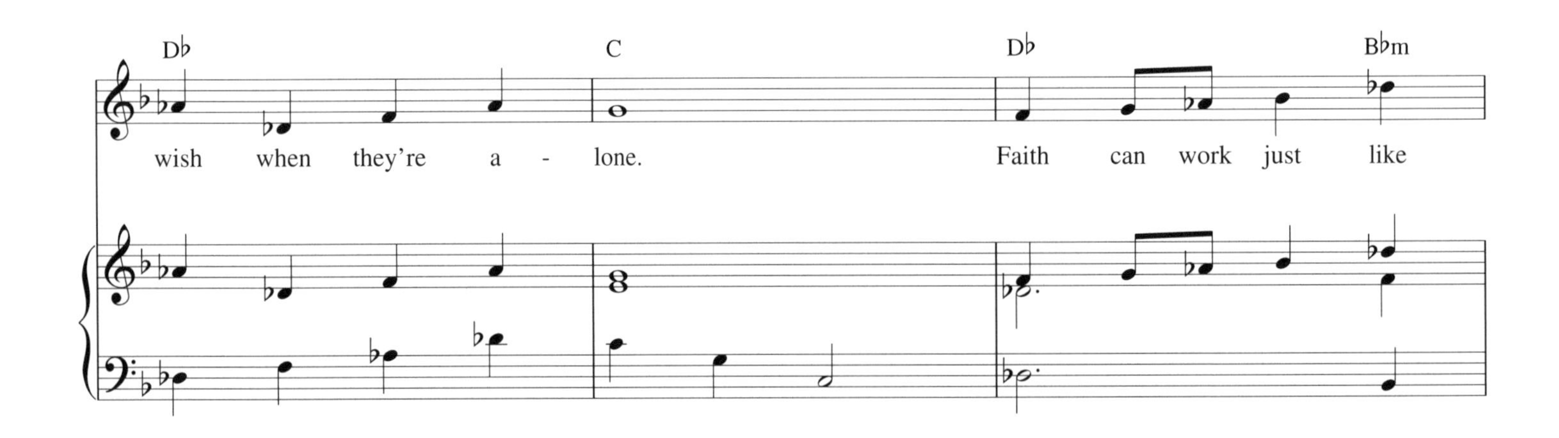

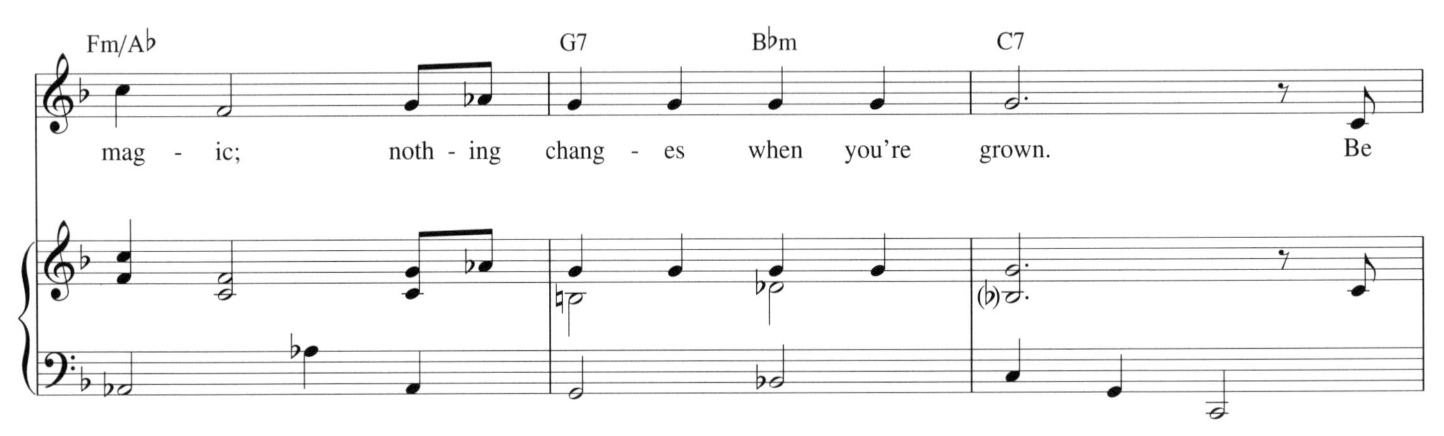

F
Gm7
B♭/C
Fmaj7
F6
brave lit - tle one
Make a wish for each sad lit - tle tear
mf (expressively)
B♭6
Am7
Dm7
G7
Hold your head up though no one is near
Some-one's wait - ing for
Gm/C
you.
Don't cry lit - tle one
Gm7
B♭/C
Fmaj7
F6
E7
There'll be a smile where a frown used to be
You'll be part of the

Am
E7
Am
love that you see
Some-one's wait - ing for you.

D7
Gm
Al - ways keep a lit - tle prayer in your pock - et and you're

D7
Gm
E7/B
sure to see the light.
Soon there'll be joy and

Am
Cm
D7
G7
B♭/C
hap - pi - ness and your lit - tle world will be bright.
Have
rit.

F
Gm7
Cm
3
Cm/B♭
faith lit - tle one 'til your hopes and your wish - es come true
3
a tempo
D7
Gm7
B♭m6
F+/A
Gm7♭5
You must try to be brave lit - tle one
Some - one's
F
F6
Gm7
C7
F
wait - ing to love you.
B♭
B♭m
F

WHEN I SEE AN ELEPHANT FLY

from Walt Disney's *Dumbo*

Words by Ned Washington
Music by Oliver Wallace

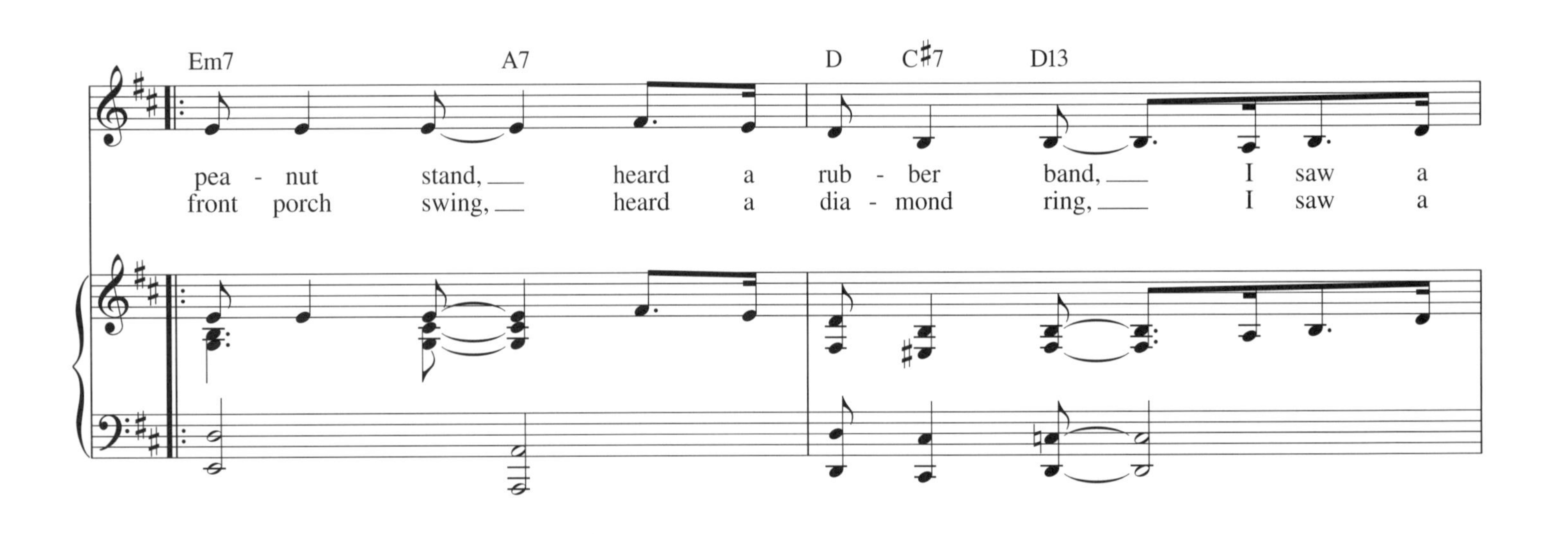

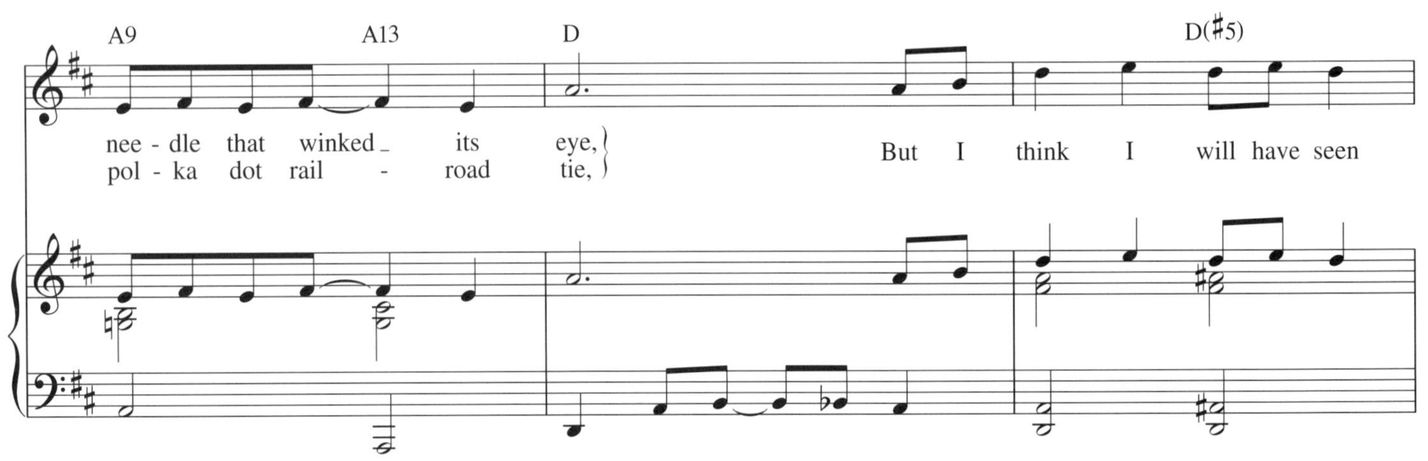

This song is performed by The Crows in the film, adapted here as a solo.

G Gm7 D E7
ev - 'ry - thing when I see an el - e-phant fly.
1
Em7 A7
I saw a
2
D D7 G Gm7
fly. I e - ven heard a choc - o - late drop, I
D/F♯ Dm/F D/E A/E♭ D D/C♯ D/C D
went in - to a store, saw a bi - cy - cle shop.
G Gm7
You can't de - ny the things that you see, But

D
B7/D♯
E7
A7
I know there's cer - tain things that just can't be. The oth - er
Em7
A7
D
C♯7
D6/B
D6/A
day by chance, saw an old barn dance, And I just
A7
A13/E
D
A7
D
D(♯5)
laughed till I thought I'd die But I think I will have seen
G/D
Gm7
D
E7
A9
D
ev - 'ry - thing When I see an el - e - phant fly.

YOU'RE NEVER FULLY DRESSED WITHOUT A SMILE

from the Musical Production *Annie*

Lyrics by Martin Charnin
Music by Charles Strouse
Arranged by Michael Dansicker

G♭Maj7 C♭7 G♭ G♭6 G°7
Beau Brum - mel - ly, They stand out a mile, But broth - er, you're
D♭7 G° D♭7 D♭9(♯5) G♭7 E♭m/G♭ B♭/G♭ G♭7
nev - er full - y dressed with - out a smile! Who
C♭ A♭m7(♭5) G♭/D♭ B♭9 E♭m G♭dim7/A
cares what they're wear - ing on Main Street or Sa - ville Row? It's what you
A♭ F7 G♭6 E♭7sus4/B♭ E♭7 A♭7 A♭13 C♭/D♭ D♭7
rit.
wear from ear to ear And not from head to toe, that mat - ters.

Stronger
D7 C/E D7/F♯ G GMaj7 G6
So Sen - a - tor, So jan - i - tor, So long for a
a tempo
E7 Am7 D7 Bm7
while. Re - mem - ber you're nev - er full - y dressed 'Tho' you may wear your
E7 Am7 D7 C/D D7
best, You're nev - er full - y dressed with - out a
E♭ E♭Maj7 E♭6 D7 G C7 G
smile, Smile, Smile, Smile, darn ya, smile!
sfz

WHERE IS LOVE?

from the Broadway Musical *Oliver!*

Words and Music by
Lionel Bart

* In the film, Oliver sings the italicized lyrics the second time.

WHO WILL BUY?

from the Broadway Musical *Oliver!*

Words and Music by
Lionel Bart

This song is performed by Oliver Twist and Chorus in the show, adapted here as a solo.

Dm
Gm7
A7
Dm
Who will tie it up with a rib - bon, and
Gm7
Gm7/C
F
put it in a box for me?
So I can
There'll nev - er
Gm
Gm7
C7♭9
Fmaj7
F6
F
F6
see it at my lei - sure when -
be a day so sun - ny; it
Gm
Gm7
C7♭9
Fmaj7
F6
ev - er things go wrong, and I would
could not hap - pen twice. Where is the

Am7 C/G F♯m7♭5 B7♭9 Em
keep it as a treas - ure to
man with all the mon - ey? It's
Am Am/G F7 E7♯5 A7♭9 A7 A7♭9 A7
last my whole life long.
cheap at half the price!
Dm Gm7 A7 Dm
Who will buy this won - der - ful feel - ing?
Gm7 Em7 A
I'm so high, I swear I could fly.

Dm
Gm7
A7
Dm
Me, oh, my, I don't want to lose it, so
Gm7
Gm7/C
F6
F7
what am I to do, to keep the sky so blue? There
B♭
A7♯5
A7
1
Dm
must be some - one who will buy.
2
Dm
Gm
Em7♭5
Dm
buy.

WITH A SMILE AND A SONG

from Walt Disney's *Snow White and the Seven Dwarfs*

Words by Larry Morey
Music by Frank Churchill

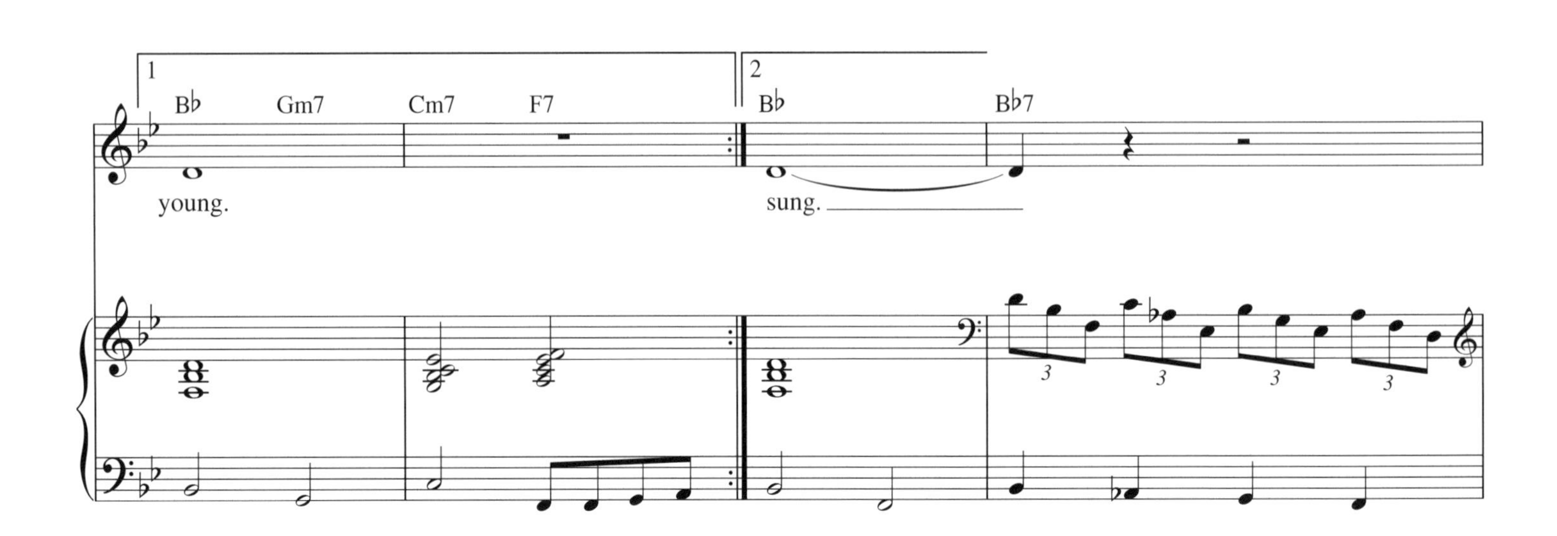

E♭ E♭m B♭6 F7 B♭ B♭m
There's no use in grum - bling, When rain - drops come tum - bling, Re -
mf
C7 Cm7 F7
mem - ber you're the one, Who can fill the world with sun - shine.
decresc.
B♭ Gm7 Cm7 F7 B♭ Gm7 Cm7 F7
When you smile and you sing, Ev - 'ry - thing is in tune and it's spring and
mp
B♭ B♭7/A♭ E♭/G F7 B♭6
rit.
life flows a - long, With a smile and a song.
rit.

WOULDN'T IT BE LOVERLY

from *My Fair Lady*

Words by Alan Jay Lerner
Music by Frederick Loewe

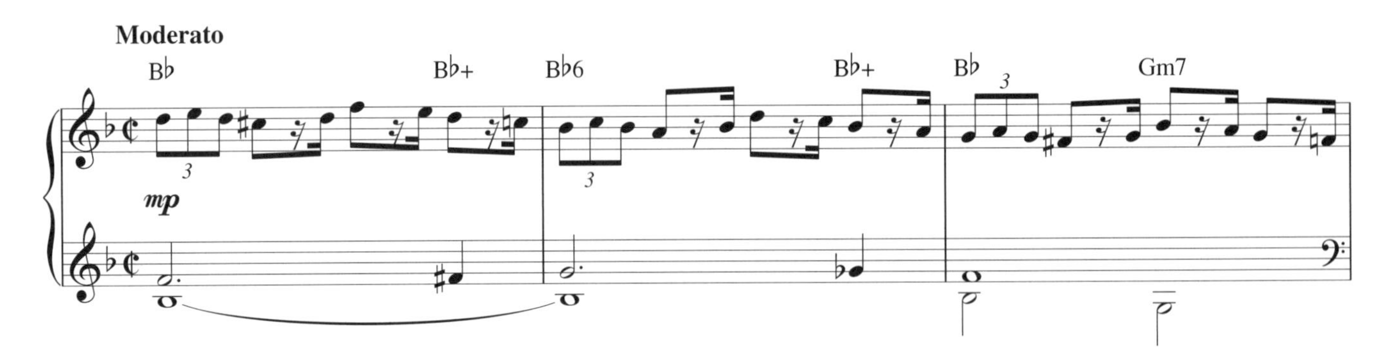

This song is performed by Eliza Doolittle and Cockneys in the show, adapted here as a solo.

Cm6/E♭ D7 B♭m/D♭ F/C Cdim Gm7/C B♭m6/C C7
nor - mous chair; Oh, would - n't it be lov - er - ly?
F B♭ Gm7 C7 F
Lots of choc' - late for me to eat; Lots of coal mak - in'
G7 C7 F C7/E Cm6/E♭ D7 B♭m/D♭
lots of heat; Warm face, warm hands, warm feet, Oh,
F/C C9 F C C♯dim7
would - n't it be lov - er - ly? Oh, so
mf

G/D
G
C
E7/B
lov - er - ly sit - tin' ab - so - bloom - in' - lute - ly
Am
E/G♯
C7/G
F6
E7
Am
E7/B
Am/C
D7
still! I would nev - er budge 'til
G
C♯dim7
Gm/C
C7
spring crept o - ver the win - dow - sill.
F
B♭
Gm7
C7
F
Some - one's head rest - in' on my knee; Warm and ten - der as

G7
C7
F
C7/E
Cm6/E♭
D7
B♭m/D♭
he can be;
Who takes good care of me. Oh,
F/C
Dm
Gm7
C7
1
F
would - n't it be lov - er - ly?
2
F
C13
F
lov - er - ly?
Lov - er - ly!
Lov - er - ly!
B♭
rall.
F
Lov - er - ly!
Lov - er - ly!
rall.
p

YOU'VE GOT A FRIEND IN ME

from Walt Disney's *Toy Story*

Music and Lyrics by
Randy Newman

F C/E E7 Am
and miles from your nice warm bed,
There is - n't an - y - thing I would - n't do for you.
F B/F♯ C/G E/G♯ Am F7 E Am D7 G7
you just re - mem - ber what your old pal said. Son, you've got a friend in me.
If we stick to - geth - er we can see it through, 'cause you've got a friend in me.
C A7 D7 G7
Yeah, you've got a friend in me.
Yeah, you've got a friend in me.
1
C E7/B
Am A♭7 C/G Cdim/G G7

2
C Cmaj7 C7
F
B
Now, some oth - er folks might be a lit - tle bit smart - er than I am,
C6 B7 C6 B C♯m7
big - ger and strong - er too. May - be. But none of them will
Ddim7 B/D♯ Em A7 Dm G7
ev - er love you the way I do, just me and you, boy.
C G7♯5 C7 F F♯dim7
And as the years go by, our friend - ship will nev - er die.

C/G
C
F
F♯dim7
C/G
E7/G♯
Am
You're gon - na see it's our des - ti - ny.
molto rit.
D7
G7
C
A7
D7
G7
You've got a friend in me.
You've got a friend in me.
a tempo
C
A7
D7
G7
C
E7/B
You've got a friend in me.
3
Am
A♭7
C/G
Cdim/G
G7
C
rit.

ZIP-A-DEE-DOO-DAH

from Walt Disney's *Song of the South*

Words by Ray Gilbert
Music by Allie Wrubel

B♭ F7 B♭ E♭ B♭
Plen - ty of sun - shine head - in' my way,
E♭ B♭ Gm Cm7 F7 B♭
Zip - a - dee - doo - dah, zip - a - dee - ay!
F7 F7/C C♯dim B♭/D
Mis - ter Blue - bird on my shoul - der,
mp
B♭ Gm7 C7
it's the truth, it's "act - ch'll,"
cresc.

F N.C.
Bb F7 Bb
Ev-'ry-thing is "sat-is-fact-ch'll." Zip-a-dee-doo-dah,
decresc.
mf
Eb Bb Eb Bb
zip-a-dee-ay! Won-der-ful feel-
Gm
1
C7 F7 Bb
-ing, won-der-ful day. Mis-ter
mp
2
C F7 Bb
won-der-ful day.
f